James Russell Lowell

Latest Literary Essays and Addresses of James Russell Lowell

James Russell Lowell

Latest Literary Essays and Addresses of James Russell Lowell

ISBN/EAN: 9783743339033

Manufactured in Europe, USA, Canada, Australia, Japa

Cover: Foto ©Thomas Meinert / pixelio.de

Manufactured and distributed by brebook publishing software (www.brebook.com)

James Russell Lowell

Latest Literary Essays and Addresses of James Russell Lowell

LATEST LITERARY ESSAYS
AND ADDRESSES

OF

JAMES RUSSELL LOWELL

BOSTON AND NEW YORK
HOUGHTON, MIFFLIN AND COMPANY
The Riverside Press, Cambridge
1892

CONTENTS.

LATEST LITERARY ESSAYS AND ADDRESSES.

GRAY.

1886.

THE eighteenth century, judged by the literature
it produced everywhere in Europe outside of Germany and France, is generally counted inferior to
that which preceded and to that which followed it.
A judgment of especial severity has been passed
upon its poetry by critics who lost somewhat of
their judicial equipoise in that enthusiasm of the
romantic reaction which replaced the goddess of
good taste by her of liberty, and crowned the judicial wig with the Phrygian cap. The poetry of the
period fell under a general condemnation as altogether wanting in the imaginative quality, and as
being rather the conclusions of the understanding
put into verse than an attempt to express, however
inadequately, the eternal longings and intuitions
and experiences of human nature. These find their
vent, it was thought, in those vivid flashes of phrase,
the instantaneous bolts of passionate conception,
whose furrow of splendor across the eyeballs of the
mind leaves them momentarily dark to the outward
universe, only to quicken their vision of inward and

incommunicable things. There was some truth in this criticism, as there commonly is in the harsh judgments of imperfect sympathy, but it was far from being the whole truth.

If poesy be, as the highest authority has defined it, a divine madness, no English poet and no French one between 1700 and 1800 need have feared a writ *de lunatico inquirendo.* They talk, to be sure, of " sacred rages," but in so decorous a tone that we do not even glance towards the tongs. They invoke fire from heaven in such frozen verse as would have set it at defiance had their prayer been answered. Cowper was really mad at intervals, but his poetry, admirable as it is in its own middle-aged way, is in need of anything rather than of a strait-waistcoat. A certain blight of propriety seems to have fallen on all the verse of that age. The thoughts, wived with words above their own level, are always on their good behavior, and we feel that they would have been happier in the homelier unconstraint of prose. Diction was expected to do for imagination what only imagination could do for it, and the magic which was personal to the magician was supposed to reside in the formula.

Dryden died with his century; and nothing can be more striking than the contrast between him, the last of the ancient line, and the new race which succeeded him. In him, too, there is an element of prose, an alloy of that good sense so admirable in itself, so incapable of those indiscretions which make the charm of poetry. His power

of continuous thinking shows his mind of a different quality from those whose thought comes as
lightning, intermittently it may be, but lightning,
mysterious, incalculable, the more unexpected that
we watch for it, and generated by forces we do
not comprehend. Yet Dryden at his best is won-
derfully impressive. He reminds one of a boiling
spring. There is tumult, concussion, and no little
vapor ; but there is force, there is abundance, there
is reverberation, and we feel that elemental fire is
at work, though it be of the earth earthy. But
what strikes us most in him, considered intellectu-
ally, is his modernness. Only twenty-three years
younger than Milton, he belongs to another world.
Milton is in many respects an ancient. Wordsworth says of him that

" His soul was a star and dwelt apart."

But I should rather be inclined to say that it was
his mind that was alienated from the present. In-
tensely and even vehemently engaged in the question of the day, his politics were abstract and
theoretic, and a quotation from Sophocles has as
much weight with him as a constitutional precedent.
His intellectual sympathies were Greek. His language even has caught the accent of the ancient
world. When he makes our English search her
coffers round, it is not for any home-made ornaments, and his commentators are fain to unravel
some of his syntax by the help of the Greek or
Latin grammar.

Dryden knew Latin literature very well, but

that innate scepticism of his mind, which made
him an admirable critic, would not allow him to be
subjugated by antiquity. His æsthetical training
was essentially French; and if this sometimes had
an ill effect on his poetry, it was greatly to the
advantage of his prose, wherein ease and dignity
are combined in that happy congruity of proportion which we call *style*, and the scholar's fulness
of mind is mercifully tempered by the man of the
world's dread of being too fiercely in earnest. It
is a gentlemanlike style, thoroughbred in every
fibre. As it was without example, so, I think, it
has remained without a parallel in English. Swift
has the ease, but lacks the lift; and Burke, who
plainly formed himself on Dryden, has matched
him in splendor, but has not caught his artistic skill
in gradation, nor that perfection of tone which can
be eloquent without being declamatory.

When I try to penetrate the secret of Dryden's
manner, I seem to discover that the new quality in
it is a certain air of good society, an urbanity, in
the original meaning of the word. By this I mean
that his turn of thought (I am speaking of his
maturer works) is that of the capital, of the great
world, as it is somewhat presumptuously called, and
that his diction is, in consequence, more conversa-
tional than that which had been traditional with
any of the more considerable poets who had preceded him. It is hard to justify a general impression by conclusive examples. Two instances will
serve to point my meaning, if not wholly to justify my generalization. His ode on the death of
Mrs. Killigrew begins thus: —

> " Thou youngest virgin-daughter of the skies,
> Made in *the last promotion* of the blest."

And in his translation of the third book of the
"Æneid," he describes Achæmenides, the Greek res-
cued by the Trojans from the island of the Cyclops,
as " bolting " from the woods.

Dryden, in making verse the vehicle of good
sense and argument rather than of passion and in-
tuition, affords but an indication of the tendency
of the time in which he lived, — a tendency quickened by the influence which could not fail to be
exerted by his really splendid powers as a poet, especially by the copious felicity of his language and
his fine instinct for the energies and harmonies of
rhythm. But the fact that a great deal of his work
was job-work, that most of it was done in a hurry,
led him often to fill up a gap with the first sonorous epithet that came to hand, and his indolence
was thus partly to blame for that poetic diction
which brought poetry to a deadlock in the next
century. Dryden knew very well that sound makes
part of the sense and a large part of the sentiment
of a verse, and, where he is in the vein, few poets
have known better than he how to conjure with
vowels, or to beguile the mind into acquiescence
through the ear. Addison said truly, though in
verses whose see-saw cadence and lack of musical
instinct would have vexed the master's ear : —

> " Great Dryden next, whose tuneful Muse affords
> The sweetest numbers and the fittest words."

But Dryden never made the discovery that ten syllables arranged in a proper accentual order were

all that was needful to make a ten-syllable verse.
He is *great* Dryden, after all, and between him and
Wordsworth there was no poet with enough energy
of imagination to deserve that epithet.   But he had
taught the trick of cadences that made the manu-
facture of verses more easy, and he had brought
the language of poetry nearer, not to the language
of real life as Wordsworth understood it, that is,
to the speech of the people, but to the language of
the educated and polite.   He himself tells us at the
end of the " Religio Laici : " —

> " And this unpolished, rugged verse I chose
>   As fittest for discourse, and nearest prose."

Unpolished and rugged the verse certainly was not,
nor in his hands could ever be.   It is the *thought*
that has an irresistible attraction for prosaic phrase,
and coalesces with it in a stubborn precipitate which
will not become ductile to the poetic form.

Dryden perfected the English rhymed heroic
verse by giving it a variety of cadence and pomp
of movement which it had never had before.
Pope's epigrammatic cast of thought led him to
spend his skill on bringing to a nicer adjustment
the balance of the couplet, in which he succeeded.
only too wearisomely well.   Between them they re-
duced versification in their favorite measure to the
precision of a mechanical art, and then came the
mob of gentlemen who wrote with ease.   Through
the whole eighteenth century the artificial school of
poetry reigned by a kind of undivine right over a
public which admired — and yawned.   This public
seems to have listened to its poets as it did to its

preachers, satisfied that all was orthodox if only they heard the same thing over again every time, and believing the pentameter couplet a part of the British Constitution. And yet it is to the credit of that age to have kept alive the wholesome tradition that Writing, whether in prose or verse, *was* an Art that required training, at least, if nothing more, in those who assumed to practise it.

Burke thought it impossible to draw an indictment against a whole people, and the remark is equally just if we apply it to a century. It is true that with the eighteenth a season of common sense set in with uncommon severity, and such a season acts like a drought upon the springs of poesy. To be sure, an unsentimental person might say that the world can get on much better without the finest verses that ever were written than without common sense, and I am willing to admit that the question is a debatable one, and to compromise upon *uncom*-mon sense whenever it is to be had. Let us admit that the eighteenth century was, on the whole, prosaic, yet it may have been a pretty fair one as centuries go. " 'T is hard to find a whole age to imitate, or what century to propose for example," says wise Sir Thomas Browne. Every age is as good as
· the people who live in it choose or can contrive to make it, and, if good enough for them, perhaps we, who had no hand in the making of it, can complain of it only so far as it had a hand in the making of us. Perhaps even our own age, with its marvels of applied science that have made the world more prosily comfortable, will loom less

gigantic than now through the prospective of the future. Perhaps it will even be found that the telephone, of which we are so proud, cannot carry human speech so far as Homer and Plato have contrived to carry it with their simpler appliances.

As one grows older, one finds more points of half-reluctant sympathy with that undyspeptic and rather worldly period, much in the same way as one grows to find a keener savor in Horace and Montaigne. In the first three quarters of it, at least, there was a cheerfulness and contentment with things as they were, which is no unsound philosophy for the mass of mankind, and which has been impossible since the first French Revolution. For our own War of Independence, though it gave the first impulse to that awful riot of human nature turned loose among first principles, was but the reassertion of established precedents and traditions, and essentially conservative in its aim, however deflected in its course. It is true that, to a certain extent, the theories of the French doctrinaires gave a tinge to the rhetoric of our patriots, but it is equally true that they did not perceptibly affect the conclusions of our Constitution-makers. Nor had those doctrinaires themselves any suspicion of the explosive mixture that can be made by the conjunction of abstract theory with brutal human instinct. Before 1789 there was a delightful period of universal confidence, during which a belief in the perfectibility of man was insensibly merging into a conviction that he could be perfected by some formula of words, just as a man is knighted. He kneels down a simple man like ourselves, is told to rise up a Perfect Being, and rises accordingly. It certainly was a comfortable time. If there was discontent, it was in the individual, and not in the air ; sporadic, not epidemic. The discomfort of Cowper was not concerning this world but the world to come. Men sate as roomily in their consciences as in the broad-bottomed chairs which suggest such solidity of repose. Responsibility for the Universe had not yet been invented. A few solitary persons saw a swarm of ominous question-marks wherever they turned their eyes ; but sensible people pronounced them the mere *muscæ volitantes* of indigestion which an honest dose of rhubarb would disperse. Men read Rousseau for amusement, and never dreamed that those flowers of rhetoric were ripening the seed of the guillotine. Post and telegraph were not so importunate as now. People were not compelled to know what all the fools in the world were saying or doing yesterday. It is impossible to conceive of a man's enjoying now the unconcerned seclusion of White at Selborne, who, a century ago, recorded the important fact that " the old tortoise at Lewes in Sussex awakened and came forth out of his dormitory," but does not seem to have heard of Burgoyne's surrender, the news of which ought to have reached him about the time he was writing. It may argue pusillanimity, but I can hardly help envying the remorseless indifference of such men to the burning questions of the hour, at the first alarm of which we are all expected to run with our buckets, or it may be with our can of kerosene, snatched by mistake in the hurry and confusion. They devoted themselves to leisure with as much assiduity as we employ to render it impossible. The art of being elegantly and strenuously idle is lost. There was no hurry then, and armies still went into winter quarters punctually as musquashes. Certainly manners occupied more time and were allowed more space. Whenever one sees a picture of that age, with its broad skirts, its rapiers standing out almost at a right angle, and demanding a wide periphery to turn about, one has a feeling of spaciousness that suggests mental as well as bodily elbow-room. Now all the ologies follow us to our burrows in our newspaper, and crowd upon us with the pertinacious benevolence of subscription-books. Even the right of sanctuary is denied. The horns of the altar, which we fain would grasp, have become those of a dilemma in the attempt to combine science with theology.

This, no doubt, is the view of a special mood, but it is a mood that grows upon us the longer we have stood upon our lees. Enough if we feel a faint thrill or reminiscence of ferment in the spring, as old wine is said to do when the grapes are in blossom. Then we are sure that we are neither dead nor turned to vinegar, and repeat softly to ourselves, in Dryden's delightful paraphrase of Horace : —

"Happy the man, and happy he alone,
    He who can call to-day his own;
    He who, secure within, can say,
'To-morrow, do thy worst, for I have lived to-day;
    Be fair or foul, or rain or shine,

The joys I have possessed in spite of Fate are mine ;
Not heaven itself upon the past has power,
But what has been, has been, and I have had my hour.' "

One has a notion that in those old times the days were longer than now ; that a man called to-day his own by a securer title, and held his hours with a sense of divine right now obsolete. It is an absurd fancy, I know, and would be sent to the right-about by the first physicist or historian you happened to meet. But one thing I am sure of, that the private person was of more importance both to himself and others then than now, and that self-consciousness was, accordingly, a vast deal more comfortable because it had less need of conscious self-assertion.

But the Past always has the advantage of us in the secret it has learned of holding its tongue, which may perhaps account in part for its reputed wisdom. Whatever the eighteenth century was, there was a great deal of stout fighting and work done in it, both physical and intellectual, and we owe it a great debt. Its very inefficacy for the higher reaches of poetry, its very good-breeding that made it shy of the raised voice and flushed features of enthusiasm, enabled it to give us the model of a domestic and drawing-room prose as distinguished from that of the pulpit, the forum, or the closet. In Germany it gave us Lessing and that half century of Goethe which made him what he was. In France it gave us Voltaire, who, if he used ridicule too often for the satisfaction of personal spite, employed it also for sixty years in the service of truth and justice, and to him more than to any other one man we owe it that we can now think and speak as we choose. Contemptible he may have been in more ways than one, but at any rate we owe him that, and it is surely something. In what is called the elegant literature of our own tongue (to speak only of the most eminent), it gave us Addison and Steele, who together made a man of genius; Pope, whose vivid genius almost persuaded wit to renounce its proper nature and become poetry; Thomson, who sought inspiration in nature, though in her least imaginative side;[1] Fielding, still in some respects our greatest novelist; Richardson, the only author who ever made long-windedness seem a benefaction; Sterne, the most subtle humorist since Shakespeare; Goldsmith, in whom the sweet humanity of Chaucer finds its nearest parallel; Cowper, the poet of Nature in her more domestic and familiar moods; Johnson, whose brawny rectitude of mind more than atones for coarseness of fibre. Toward the middle of the century, also, two books were published which made an epoch in æsthetics, Dodsley's "Old Plays" (1744) and Percy's "Ballads" (1765). These gave the first impulse to the romantic reaction against a miscalled classicism, and were the seed of the literary renaissance.

The temper of the times and the comfortable conditions on which life was held by the educated

---

[1] That Thomson was a man of true poetic sensibility is shown, I think, more agreeably in *The Castle of Indolence* than in *The Seasons*. In these, when he buckles the buskins of Milton on the feet of his natural *sermo pedestris*, the effect too often suggests the unwieldy gait of a dismounted trooper in his jack-boots.

class were sure to produce a large crop of dilettante-ism, of delight in art and the things belonging to it as an elegant occupation of the mind without taxing its faculties too severely. If the dilettante in his eagerness to escape ennui sometimes become a bore himself, especially to the professional artist, he is not without his use in keeping alive the traditions of good taste and transmitting the counsels of experience. In proportion as his critical faculty grows sensitive, he becomes incapable of production himself. For indeed his eye is too often trained rather to detect faults than excellences, and he can tell you where and how a thing differs for the worse from established precedent, but not where it differs for the better. This habit of mind would make him distrustful of himself and sterile in original production, for his consciousness of how much can be said against whatever is done and even well done reacts upon him and makes him timid. It is the rarest thing to find genius and dilettanteism united in the same person (as for a time they were in Goethe). for genius implies always a certain fanaticism of temperament, which, if sometimes it seem fitful, is yet capable of intense energy on occasion, while the main characteristic of the dilettante is that sort of impartiality which springs from inertia of mind, admirable for observation, incapable of turning it to practical account. Yet we have, I think, an example of this rare combination of qualities in Gray, and it accounts both for the kind of excellence to which he attained, and for the way in which he disappointed expectation, his own,

I suspect, first of all. He is especially interesting as an artist in words and phrases, a literary type far less common among writers of English, than it is in France or Italy, where perhaps the traditions of Latin culture were never wholly lost, or, even if they were, continued to be operative by inheritance through the form they had impressed upon the mind. Born in 1716, he died in his 55th year, leaving behind him hardly fourteen hundred verses. Dante was one year older, Shakespeare, three years younger when he died. It seems a slender monument, yet it has endured and is likely to endure, so close-grained is the material and so perfect the workmanship. When so many have written too much, we shall the more readily pardon the rare man who has written too little or just enough.

The incidents of Gray's life are few and unimportant. Educated at Eton and diseducated, as he seemed to think, at Cambridge, in his twenty-third year he was invited by Horace Walpole to be his companion in a journey to Italy. At the end of two years they quarrelled, and Gray returned to England. Dr. Johnson has explained the causes of this rupture, with his usual sturdy good sense and knowledge of human nature: " Mr. Walpole," he says, " is now content to have it told that it was by his fault. If we look, however, without prejudice on the world, we shall find that men whose consciousness of their own merit sets them above the compliances of servility, are apt enough in their association with superiors to watch their own dignity with troublesome and punctilious jealousy, and in

the fervor of independence to exact that attention
which they refuse to pay." Johnson was obeying
Sidney's prescription of looking into his own heart
when he wrote that. Walpole's explanation is of
the same purport: " I was young, too fond of my
own diversion ; nay, I do not doubt too much in-
toxicated by indulgence, vanity, and the insolences
of my situation as a Prime Minister's son. . . . I
treated him insolently. . . . Forgive me if I say
that his temper was not conciliating." They were
reconciled a few years later and continued cour-
teously friendly till Gray's death. A meaner explanation of their quarrel has been given by gossip;
that a letter which Gray had written home was
opened and read by Walpole, who found in it something not to his own advantage. But the reconcilia-
tion sufficiently refutes this, for if Gray could have
consented to overlook the baseness, Walpole could
never have forgiven its detection.

Gray was a conscientious traveller, as the notes
he has left behind him prove. One of these, on
the Borghese Gallery at Rome, is so characteristic
as to be worth citing: " Several (Madonnas) of
Rafael, Titian, Andrea del Sarto, etc., but in none
of them all that heavenly grace and beauty that
Guido gave, and that Carlo Maratt has so well imitated in subjects of this nature." This points to
an admission which those who admire Gray, as I do,
are forced to make, sooner or later, that there was
a tint of effeminacy in his nature. That he should
have admired Norse poetry, Ossian, and the Scot-
tish ballads is not inconsistent with this, but may

be explained by what is called the attraction of opposites, which means merely that we are wont to overvalue qualities or aptitudes which we feel to be wanting in ourselves. Moreover these anti-classical yearnings of Gray began after he had ceased producing, and it was not unnatural that he should admire men who did without thinking what he could not do by taking thought. Elegance, sweetness, pathos, or even majesty he could achieve, but never that force which vibrates in every verse of larger-moulded men.

Bonstetten tells us that "every sensation in Gray was passionate," but I very much doubt whether he was capable of that sustained passion of the mind which is fed by a prevailing imagination acting on the consciousness of great powers. That was something he could never feel, though he knew what it meant by his observation of others, and longed to feel it. In him imagination was passive; it could divine and select, but not create. Bonstetten, after seeing the best society in Europe on equal terms, also tells us that Gray was the most finished gentleman he had ever seen. Is it over fine to see something ominous in that word *finished?* It seems to imply limitations; to imply a consciousness that sees everything between it and the goal rather than the goal itself, that undermines enthusiasm through the haunting doubt of being undermined. We cannot help feeling in the poetry of Gray that it too is finished, perhaps I should rather say limited, as the greatest things never are, as it is one of their merits that they never can be.

They suggest more than they bestow, and enlarge our apprehension beyond their own boundaries. Gray shuts us in his own contentment like a cathedral close or college quadrangle. He is all the more interesting, perhaps, that he was a true child of his century, in which decorum was religion. He could not, as Dryden calls it in his generous way, give his soul a loose, although he would. He is of the eagle brood, but unfledged. His eye shares the æther which shall never be cloven by his wing.

But it is one of the school-boy blunders in criticism to deny one kind of perfection because it is not another. Gray, more than any of our poets, has shown what a depth of sentiment, how much pleasurable emotion, mere words are capable of stirring through the magic of association, and of artful arrangement in conjunction with agreeable and familiar images. For Gray is pictorial in the highest sense of the term, much more than imaginative. Some passages in his letters give us a hint that he might have been. For example, he asks his friend Stonehewer, in 1760, " Did you never observe (*while rocking winds are piping loud*) that pause as the gust is re-collecting itself?" But in his verse there is none of that intuitive phrase where the imagination at a touch precipitates thought, feeling, and image in an imperishable crystal. He knew imagination when he saw it; no man better; he could have scientifically defined it; but it would not root in the artificial soil of his own garden, though he transplanted a bit now and then. Here is an instance: Dryden in his " Annus Mirabilis,"

hinting that Louis XIV. would fain have joined
Holland against England, if he dared, says : —

> " And threatening France, placed like a painted Jove,
>   Held idle thunder in his lifted hand.''

Gray felt how fine this was, and makes his
Agrippina say that it was she

> "that armed
> This painted Jove and taught his novice hand
> To aim the forked bolt, while he stood trembling,
> Scared at the sound and dazzled with its brightness.''

Pretty well, one would say, for a "*painted* Jove"!
The imagination is sometimes *super grammaticam*,
like the Emperor Sigismund, but it is coherent by
the very law of its being.[1]

Gray brought home from France and Italy a
familiar knowledge of their languages, and that enlarged culture of the eye which is one of the insen-
sible, as it is one of the greatest gains of travel.
The adventures he details in his letters are generally such as occur to all the world, but there is
a passage in one of them in which he describes a
scene at Rheims in 1739, so curious and so characteristic of the time as to be worth citing : —

> " The other evening we happened to be got together
> in a company of eighteen people, men and women of the
> best fashion here, at a garden in the town to walk ; when
> one of the ladies bethought herself of asking 'Why
> should not we sup here ? ' Immediately the cloth was

---

[1] It is always interesting to trace the germs of lucky phrases.
Dryden was familiar with the works of Beaumont and Fletcher,
and it may be suspected that this noble image was suggested by a
verse in *The Double Marriage* — " Thou woven Worthy in a piece
of arras."

laid by the side of a fountain under the trees. and a very
elegant supper served up ; after which another said,
'Come, let us sing,' and directly began herself ; from
singing we insensibly fell to dancing and singing in a
round, when somebody mentioned the violins, and immediately a company of them was ordered. Minuets were
begun in the open air, and then came country dances
which held till four o'clock in the morning, at which
hour the gayest lady there proposed that such as were
weary should get into their coaches, and the rest . . .
should dance before them with the music in the van ;
and in this manner we paraded through the principal
streets of the city and waked everybody in it."

This recalls the garden of Boccaccio, and if it be
hard to fancy the " melancholy Gray " leading off
such a jig of Comus, it is almost harder to conceive
that this was only fifty years before the French
Revolution. And yet it was precisely this gay
insouciance, this forgetfulness that the world existed for any but a single class in it, and this care-
lessness of the comfort of others that made the
catastrophe possible.

Immediately on his return he went back to Cambridge, where he spent (with occasional absences)
the rest of his days, first at Peter House and then
at Pembroke College. In 1768, three years before
his death, he was appointed professor of Modern
Literature and Languages, but he never performed
any of its functions except that of receiving the
salary — " so did the Muse defend her son." Johnson describes him as " always designing lectures,
but never reading them ; uneasy at his neglect of

duty and appeasing his uneasiness with designs of reformation and with a resolution, which he believed himself to have made, of resigning the office, if he found himself unable to discharge it." This is excellently well divined, for nobody knew better than Johnson what a master of casuistry is indolence, but I find no trace of any such feeling in Gray's correspondence. After the easy-going fashion of his day he was more likely to consider his salary as another form of pension.

The first poem of Gray that was printed was the " Ode on the Distant Prospect of Eton College," and this when he was already thirty-one. The " Elegy " followed in 1750, the other lesser odes in 1753, " The Progress of Poesy " and the " Bard " in 1757. Collins had preceded him in this latter species of composition, a man of more original imagination and more fervent nature, but inferior in artistic instinct. Mason gives a droll reason for the success of the " Elegy : " " It spread at first on account of the affecting and pensive cast of the subject — just like Hervey's ' Meditations on the Tombs.' " What Walpole called Gray's flowering period ended with his fortieth year. From that time forward he wrote no more. Twelve years later, it is true, he writes to Walpole : —

"What has one to do, when turned of fifty, but really to think of finishing? . . . However, I will be candid . . . and avow to you that, till fourscore and ten, whenever the humor takes me, I will write because I like it, and because I like myself better when I do so. If I do not write much it is because I cannot."

Chaucer was growing plumper over his " Canterbury Tales," and the " Divina Commedia " was still making Dante leaner, when both those poets were "turned of fifty." Had Milton pleaded the same discharge, we should not have had " Paradise Lost " and " Samson Agonistes."

No doubt Gray could have written more " if he had set himself doggedly about it," as Johnson has recommended in such cases, but he never did, and I suspect that it was this neglect rather than that of his lectures that irked him. The words " *because I like myself better when I do* " seem to point in that direction. Bonstetten, who knew him a year later than the date of this letter, says : —

"The poetical genius of Gray was so extinguished in the gloomy residence of Cambridge that the recollection of his poems was hateful to him. He never permitted me to speak to him about them. When I quoted some of his verses to him, he held his tongue like an obstinate child. I said to him sometimes, ' Will you not answer me, then ? ' but no word came from his lips. I saw him every evening from five o'clock till midnight. We read Shakespeare, whom he adored, Dryden, Pope, Milton, etc., and our conversations, like those of friendship, knew no end. I told Gray about my life and my country, but all his own life was shut from me. Never did he speak of himself. There was in Gray between the present and the past an impassable abyss. When I would have approached it, gloomy clouds began to cover it. I believe that Gray had never loved; this was the key to the riddle."

One cannot help wishing that Bonstetten had

Boswellized some of these endless conversations, for the talk of Gray was, on the testimony of all who heard it, admirable for fulness of knowledge, point, and originality of thought. Sainte-Beuve, commenting on the words of Bonstetten, says, with his usual quick insight and graceful cleverness: —

"Je ne sais si Bonstetten avait deviné juste et si le secret de la mélancolie de Gray était dans ce manque d'amour; je le chercherais plutôt dans la stérilité d'un talent poétique si distingué, si rare, mais si avare. Oh! comme je le comprends mieux, dans ce sens-là, le silence obstiné et boudeur des poëtes profonds, arrivés à un certain âge et taris, cette rancune encore aimante envers ce qu'on a tant aimé et qui ne reviendra plus, cette douleur d'une âme orpheline de poésie et qui ne veut pas être consolée!"

But Sainte-Beuve was thinking rather of the author of a certain volume of French poetry published under the pseudonym of Joseph Delorme than of Gray. Gray had been a successful poet, if ever there was one, for he had pleased both the few and the many. There is a great difference between I could if I would and I would if I could in their effect on the mind. Sainte-Beuve is perhaps partly right, but it may be fairly surmised that the remorse for intellectual indolence should have had some share in making Gray unwilling to recall the time when he was better employed than in filling-in coats-of-arms on the margin of Dugdale and correcting the Latin of Linnæus. I suspect that his botany, his heraldry, and his weather-calendars were mere expedients to make himself believe he was doing something, and that he might have an excuse ready when conscience reproached him with *not* doing something he could do better. He speaks of "his natural indolence and indisposition to act," in a letter to Wharton. Temple tells us that he wished rather to be looked on as a gentleman than as a man of letters, and this may have been partly true at a time when authorship was still lodged in Grub Street and in many cases deserved no better. Gray had the admirable art of making himself respected by beginning first himself. He always treated Thomas Gray with the distinguished consideration he deserved. Perhaps neither Bonstetten nor Sainte-Beuve was precisely the man to understand the more than English reserve of Gray, the reserve of a man as proud as he was sensitive. And Gray's pride was not, as it sometimes is, allied to vanity; it was personal rather than social, if I may attempt a distinction which I feel but can hardly define. After he became famous, one of the several Lords Gray claimed kindred with him, perhaps I should say was willing that *he* should claim it, on the ground of a similarity of arms. Gray preferred his own private distinction, and would not admit their lordships to any partnership in it. Michael Angelo, who fancied himself a proud man, was in haste to believe a purely imaginary pedigree that derived him from the Counts of Canossa.

That I am right in saying that Gray's melancholy was in part remorse at (if I may not say the waste) the abeyance of his powers, may be read between the lines (I think) in more than one of his letters. His constant endeavor was to occupy himself in whatever would save him from the reflection of how he might occupy himself better. "To find one's self business," he says, " (I am persuaded), is the great art of life. . . . Some spirit, some genius (more than common) is required to teach a man how to employ himself." And elsewhere : "to be employed is to be happy," which was a saying he borrowed of Swift, another self-dissatisfied man. Bonstetten says in French that " his mind was gay and his character melancholy." In German he substitutes " soul" for "character." He was cheerful, that is, in any company but his own, and this, it may be guessed, because faculties were called into play which he had not the innate force to rouse into more profitable activity. Gray's melancholy was that of Richard II. : —

> " I wasted time, and now doth time waste me,
> For now hath time made me his numbering-clock."

Whatever the cause, it began about the time when he had finally got his two great odes off his hands. At first it took the form of resignation, as when he writes to Mason in 1757 : —

> " I can only tell you that one who has far more reason than you, I hope, will ever have to look on life with something worse than indifference, is yet no enemy to it, but can look backward on many bitter moments, partly with satisfaction, and partly with patience, and forward, too, on a scene not very promising, with some hope and some expectation of a better day."

But it is only fair to give his own explanation of

his unproductiveness. He writes to Wharton, who had asked him for an epitaph on a child just lost : —

"I by no means pretend to inspiration, but yet I affirm that the faculty in question is by no means voluntary. It is the result, I suppose, of a certain disposition of mind which does not depend on one's self, and which I have not felt this long time."

In spite of this, however, it should be remembered that the motive power always becomes sluggish in men who too easily admit the supremacy of moods. But an age of common sense would very greatly help such a man as Gray to distrust himself.

If Gray ceased to write poetry, let us be thankful that he continued to write letters. Cowper, the poet, a competent judge, for he wrote excellent letters himself, and therefore had studied the art, says, writing to Hill in 1777 : —

" I once thought Swift's letters the best that could be written ; but I like Gray's better. His humor, or his wit, or whatever it is to be called, is never ill-natured or offensive, and yet, I think, equally poignant with the Dean's."

I think the word that Cowper was at a loss for was *playfulness*, the most delightful ingredient in letters, for Gray can hardly be said to have had humor in the deeper sense of the word. The nearest approach to it I remember is where he writes (as Lamb would have written) to Walpole suffering with the gout: " The pain in your feet I can bear. " He has the knack of saying droll things in an off-hand way, and as if they cost him nothing. It is only the most delicately trained hand that can venture on this playful style, easy as it seems, without danger of a catastrophe, and Gray's perfect elegance could nowhere have found a more admirable foil than in the vulgar jauntiness and clumsy drollery of his correspondent, Mason. Let me cite an example or two.

He writes to Wharton, 1753 : —

"I take it ill you should say anything against the Mole. It is a reflection, I see, cast at the Thames. Do you think that rivers which have lived in London and its neighbourhood all their days will run roaring and tumbling about like your tramontane torrents in the North ?"

To Brown, 1767 : —

" Pray that the Trent may not intercept us at Newark, for we have had infinite rain here, and they say every brook sets up for a river."

Of the French, he writes to Walpole, in Paris : —

"I was much entertained with your account of our neighbours. As an Englishman and an anti-Gallican, I rejoice at their dulness and their nastiness, though I fear we shall come to imitate them in both. Their atheism is a little too much, too shocking to be rejoiced at. I have long been sick at it in their authors and hated them for it; but I pity their poor innocent people of fashion. They were bad enough when they believed everything."

Of course it is difficult to give instances of a thing in its nature so evanescent, yet so subtly pervasive, as what we call *tone*. I think it is in this, if in anything, that Gray's letters are on the whole superior to Swift's. This playfulness of Gray very easily becomes tenderness on occasion, and even pathos.

Writing to his friend Nicholls in 1765, he says:

"It is long since I heard you were gone in haste into Yorkshire on account of your mother's illness, and the same letter informed me she was recovered. Otherwise I had then wrote to you only to beg you would take care of her, and to inform you that I had discovered a thing very little known, which is, that in one's whole life one can never have any more than a single mother. You may think this obvious and (what you call) a trite observation. . . . You are a green gosling! I was at the same age (very near) as wise as you, and yet I never discovered this (with full evidence and conviction. I mean) till it was too late. It is thirteen years ago and it seems but as yesterday, and every day I live it sinks deeper into my heart."

In his letters of condolence, perhaps the most arduous species of all composition, Gray shows the same exquisite tact which is his distinguishing characteristic as a poet. And he shows it by never attempting to console. Perhaps his notions on this matter may be divined in what he writes to Walpole about Lyttelton's " Elegy on his Wife : " —

"I am not totally of your mind as to Mr. Lyttelton's elegy, though I love kids and fawns as little as you do. If it were all like the fourth stanza I should be excessively pleased. Nature and sorrow and tenderness are the true genius of such things; and something of these I find in several parts of it (not in the orange tree);

poetical ornaments are foreign to the purpose, for they only show a man is not sorry; and devotion worse, for it teaches him that he ought not to be sorry, which is all the pleasure of the thing."

And to Mason he writes in September, 1753 : —

"I know what it is to lose a person that one's eyes and heart have long been used to, and I never desire to part with the remembrance of that loss."　(His mother died in the March of that year.)

Gray's letters also are a mine of acute observation and sharply-edged criticism upon style, especially those to Mason and Beattie.　His *obiter dicta* have the weight of wide reading and much reflection by a man of delicate apprehension and tenacious memory for principles.　" Mr. Gray used to say," Mason tells us, "that good writing not only required great parts, but the very best of those parts." [1]　I quote a few of his sayings almost at random : —

" Have you read Clarendon's book ?　Do you remember Mr. Cambridge's account of it before it came out ? How well he recollected all the faults, and how utterly he forgot all the beauties ?　Surely the grossest taste is better than such a sort of delicacy."

"I think even a bad verse as good a thing or better than the best observation that ever was made upon it."

---

[1] This, perhaps, suggested to Coleridge his admirable definition of the distinction between the language of poetry and of prose.　It is almost certain that Coleridge learned from Gray his nicety in the use of vowel-sounds and the secret that in a verse it is the letter that giveth life quite as often as the spirit.　Many poets have been intuitively lucky in the practice of this art, but Gray had formulated it.

" Half a word fixed upon or near the spot is worth a
cart-load of recollection." (He is speaking of descrip-
tions of scenery, but what he says is of wider application.)

" Froissart is the Herodotus of a barbarous age."

" Jeremy Taylor is the Shakespeare of divines."

" I rejoice when I see Machiavel defended or illustrated, who to me appears one of the wisest men that
any nation in any age has produced."

" In truth, Shakespeare's language is one of his prin-
·cipal beauties, and he has no less advantage over your
Addisons and Rowes in this than in those other great
excellencies you mention. Every word in him is a picture."

Of Dryden he said to Beattie : —

" That if there was any excellence in his own num-
bers he had learned it wholly from that great poet, and
pressed him with great earnestness to study, as his
choice of words and [his] versification were singularly
happy and harmonious."

And again he says in a postscript to Beattie : —

" Remember Dryden, and be blind to all his faults."

To Mason he writes : —

" All I can say is that your ' Elegy ' must not end with
the worst line in it ; it is flat, it is prose ; whereas that,
above all, ought to sparkle, or at least to shine. If the
sentiment must stand, twirl it a little into an apothegm,
stick a flower in it, gild it with a costly expression ; let
it strike the fancy, the ear, or the heart, and I am
satisfied."

Gray and Mason together, however, could not
make the latter a poet !

"Now I insist that sense is nothing in poetry, but according to the dress she wears and the scene she appears in."

"I have got the old Scotch ballad on which 'Douglas' [Home's] was founded; it is divine, and as long as from hence to Ashton. Have you never seen it? Aristotle's best rules are observed in it in a manner that shows the author never had heard of Aristotle."

"This latter [speaking of a passage in 'Caractacus'] is exemplary for the expression (always the great point with me); I do not mean by expression the mere choice of words, but the whole dress, fashion, and arrangement of a thought."

"Extreme conciseness of expression, yet pure, perspicuous, and musical, is one of the grand beauties of lyric poetry; this I have always aimed at and never could attain."

Of his own Agrippina he says : —

"She seemed to me to talk like an old boy all in figures and mere poetry, instead of nature and the language of real passion."

Of the minuteness of his care in matters of expression an example or two will suffice. Writing to Mason he says : —

"Sure 'seers' comes over too often; besides, it sounds ill." "Plann'd is a nasty stiff word." "I cannot give up 'lost' for it begins with an *l*."

Yet Gray's nice ear objected to "*vain vision*" as hard.

It may be asked if those minutiæ of alliteration and of close or open vowel-sounds are consistent with anything like that ecstasy of mind, from

which the highest poetry is supposed to spring,
and which it is its function to reproduce in the
mind of the reader. But whoever would write
well must *learn* to write. Shelley was almost as
great a corrector of his own verses as Pope. Even
in Shakespeare we can trace the steps and even the
models by which he arrived at that fatality of
phrase which seems like immediate inspiration.
One at least of the objects of writing is (or was)
to be read, and, other things being equal, the best
writers are those who make themselves most easily
readable. Gray's great claim to the rank he holds
is derived from his almost unrivalled skill as an
artist, in words and sounds; as an artist, too, who
knew how to compose his thoughts and images
with a thorough knowledge of perspective. This
explains why he is so easy to remember; why,
though he wrote so little, so much of what he
wrote is familiar on men's tongues. There are
certain plants that have seeds with hooks by which
they cling to any passing animal and impress his
legs into the service of their locomotion and distribution. Gray's phrases have the same gift of
hooking themselves into the memory, and it was
due to the exquisite artifice of their construc-
tion. His "Elegy," certainly not through any
originality of thought, but far more through originality of sound, has charmed all ears from the day
it was published; and the measure in which it is
written, though borrowed by Gray of Dryden, by
Dryden of Davenant, by Davenant of Davies, and
by him of Raleigh, is ever since associated with

that poem as if by some exclusive right of property. ˙ Perhaps the great charm of the "Elegy" is to be found in its embodying that pensively sting-less pessimism which comes with the first gray hair; that vague sympathy with ourselves, which is so much cheaper than sympathy with others ; that placid melancholy which satisfies the general appetite for an emotion which titillates rather than wounds.

The "Progress of Poesy" and "The Bard" made their way more slowly, though the judgment of the elect (the δυνατοί to whom Gray proudly appealed) placed them at the head of English lyric poetry. By the majority they were looked on as divine in the sense that they were past all understanding. Goldsmith criticised them in the "Monthly Review," and a few passages of his article are worth quoting as coming from him : —

"We cannot, however, without some regret, behold those talents so capable of giving pleasure to all, exerted in efforts that, at best, can amuse only the few; we cannot behold this rising poet seeking fame among the learned, without hinting to him the same advice that Isocrates used to give his pupils, ' Study the people.' . . . He speaks to a people not easily impressed with new ideas; extremely tenacious of the old; with difficulty warmed and as slowly cooling again. How unsuited, then, to our national character is that species of poetry which rises on us with unexpected flights ; where we must hastily catch the thought or it flies from us ; and in short, where the reader must largely partake of the poet's enthusiasm in order to taste his beauties ! . . . These two odes, it must be confessed, breathe much of the spirit of Pindar; but then they have caught the seeming obscurity, the sudden transition and hazardous epithet of the mighty master, all which, though evidently intended for beauties, will probably be regarded as blemishes by the generality of readers. In short, they are in some measure a representation of what Pindar now appears to be, though perhaps not what he appeared to the States of Greece."

Goldsmith preferred " The Bard " to the " Progress of Poesy." We seem to see him willing to praise and yet afraid to like. He is possessed by the true spirit of his age. For my part I think I see as much influence of the Italian " Canzone " as of Pindar in these odes. Nor would they be better for being more like Pindar. Ought not a thing once thoroughly well done to be left conscientiously alone? And was it not Gray's object that these odes should have something of the same inspiring effect on English-speaking men as those others on Greek-speaking men? To give the same lift to the fancy and feeling? Goldsmith unconsciously gave them the right praise when he said they had "caught the spirit" of the elder poet. I remember hearing Emerson say some thirty years ago, that he valued Gray chiefly as a comment on Pindar.

Gray himself seems to have kept his balance very well; indeed, it may be conjectured that he knew the shortcomings of his work better than any one else could have told him of them. He writes to Hurd : —

"As your acquaintance in the University (you say)

do me the honor to admire, it would be ungenerous
in me not to give them notice that they are doing a
very unfashionable thing, for all People of Condition
are agreed not to admire, nor even to understand. One
very great man, writing to an acquaintance of his and
mine, says that he had read them seven or eight times,
and that now, when he next sees him, he shall not
have above thirty questions to ask. Another, a peer,
believes that the last stanza of the second Ode relates to
King Charles the First and Oliver Cromwell. Even
my friends tell me they do not succeed, and write me
moving topics of consolation on that head. In short, I
have heard of nobody but an actor and a Doctor of Divinity that profess their esteem for them. Oh yes, a lady
of quality (a friend of Mason's), who is a great reader.
She knew there was a compliment to Dryden, but never
suspected there was anything said about Shakespeare
and Milton, till it was explained to her; and wishes that
there had been titles prefixed to tell what they were
about."

If the success of the Odes was not such as to en-
courage Gray to write more, they certainly added
to his fame and made their way to admiration in
France and Italy.

The fate of Gray since his death has been a
singular one. He has been underrated both by
the Apostles of Common Sense and of Imagination, by Johnson, and Wordsworth. Johnson was
in an uncommonly surly mood even for him when
he wrote his life of Gray. He blames and praises
him for the same thing. He makes it a fault in
the " Ode on the Distant Prospect of Eton College,"
that " the prospect . . . suggests nothing to Gray

which every beholder does not equally think and feel ; " and a merit of the " Elegy," that " it abounds with images which find a mirror in every mind, and with sentiments to which every bosom returns an echo." This no doubt is one of the chief praises of Gray, as of other poets, that he is the voice of emotions common to all mankind. " Tell me what I feel," is what everybody asks of the poet. But surely it makes some difference *how* we are told. It is one proof how good a thing is that it looks so easy after it is done. Johnson growls also at Mr. Walpole's cat, as if he were one of the race which is the hereditary foe of that animal. He hits a blot when he criticises " the azure flowers that blow," but is blind to the easy fancy, the almost feline grace of the whole, with its playful claws of satire sheathed in velvet.

Wordsworth in his famous Preface attacks Gray as " the head of those who by their reasonings have attempted to widen the space of separation betwixt prose and metrical composition " [he means betwixt the language of the two], " and was more than any other man curiously elaborate in the structure of his own poetic diction." He then quotes Gray's sonnet on the death of his friend West.

" In vain to me the smiling mornings shine,
   And reddening Phœbus lifts his golden fire ;
   The birds in vain their amorous descant join,
   Or cheerful fields resume their green attire ;
   These ears, alas. for other notes repine,
   A different object do these eyes require :
   My lonely anguish melts no heart but mine ;
   And in my breast the imperfect joys expire.

> Yet morning smiles the busy race to cheer,
> And newborn pleasure springs to happier men;
> The fields to all their wonted tribute bear;
> To warm their little loves the birds complain;
> *I fruitless mourn to him that cannot hear,*
> *And weep the more because I weep in vain."*

"It will easily be perceived that the only part of
this sonnet which is of any value is the lines printed
in italics; it is equally obvious that except in the
rhyme and in the use of the single word 'fruit-
less' for 'fruitlessly,' which is so far a defect, the
language of these lines does in no respect differ
from that of prose." I think this criticism a little
ungracious, for it would not be easy to find many
sonnets (even of Wordsworth's own) with five
first-rate verses out of the fourteen. But what is
most curious is that Wordsworth should not have
seen that this very sonnet disproves the theory of
diction with which he charges him. I cannot find
that he had any such theory. He does, indeed, say
somewhere that the language of the age is never
the language of poetry, which if taken as he understood it is true, but I know not where Wordsworth
found his "reasonings." Gray by the language
of the age meant the language of conversation,
for he goes on to say, "Except among the French,
whose verse, where the thought or image does not
support it, differs in nothing from prose." Gray's
correspondence with Mason proves that he had no
such theory. Let a pair of instances suffice.

"There is an affectation in so often using the
old phrase 'or ere' for 'before.'" "*Intellect* is
a word of science and therefore inferior to any

more common word." Wordsworth should have
had more sympathy with a man who loved mountains as well as he, and not wholly in the eighteenth-
century fashion either. "Not a precipice, not a
torrent, not a cliff," writes Gray from the Grande
Chartreuse, "but is pregnant with religion and
poetry." That was Wordsworth's own very view,
his ownty-downty view one is sometimes tempted
to call it, when he won't let anybody else have a
share in it.

After a journey in Scotland : —

"The Lowlands are worth seeing once, but the mountains are ecstatic and ought to be visited in pilgrimage
once a year. None but those monstrous creatures of God
know how to join so much beauty with so much horror.
A fig for your poets, painters, gardeners, and clergymen
that have not been among them ; their imagination can
be made up of nothing but bowling-greens, flowering-
shrubs, horse-ponds, Fleet-ditches, shell-grottoes, and
Chinese rails."

Sir James Mackintosh says that Gray first traced
out every picturesque tour in Britain, and Gray
was a perpetual invalid. He discovered the Wye
before Wordsworth, and floated down it in a boat,
"near forty miles, surrounded with ever-new delights ; " nay, it was he who made known the Lake
region to the Lakers themselves. Wordsworth, I
can't help thinking, had a little unconscious jealousy of Gray, whose fame as the last great poet
was perhaps somewhat obtrusive when Wordsworth was at the University. His last word about
him is in a letter to Gillies in 1816.

"Gray failed as a poet not because he took too much pains and so extinguished his animation, but because he had very little of that fiery quality to begin with, and his pains were of the wrong sort. He wrote English verses as his brother Eton schoolboys wrote Latin, filching a phrase now from one author and now from another. I do not profess to be a person of very various reading; nevertheless, if I were to pluck out of Gray's tail all of the feathers which I know belong to other birds, he would be left very bare indeed. Do not let anybody persuade you that any quantity of good verses can be produced by mere felicity; or that an immortal style can be the growth of mere genius. '*Multa tulit fecitque*' must be the motto of all those who are to last." [1]

What would be left to Gray after this plucking would be his genius, for genius he certainly had, or he could not have produced the effect of it. The gentle Cowper, no bad critic also he, was kinder.

"I have been reading Gray's works," he says, "and think him the only poet since Shakespeare entitled to the character of sublime. Perhaps you will remember that I once had a different opinion of him. I was prejudiced."

In spite of unjust depreciation and misapplied criticism, Gray holds his own and bids fair to last

---

[1] I need not point out that Wordsworth is a little confused, if not self-contradictory in this criticism. I will add only two quotations to show that accidents will happen to the best-regulated poets : —

"At distance heard the murmur of many waterfalls not audible in the day-time." — Gray to Wharton, 1769.

> "A soft and lulling sound is heard
> Of streams inaudible by day." — *White Doe.*

Gray probably guided Wordsworth to the vein of gold in Dyer.

as long as the language which he knew how to write
so well and of which he is one of the glories.
Wordsworth is justified in saying that he helped
himself from everybody and everywhere — and yet
he made such admirable use of what he stole (if
theft there was) that we should as soon think of
finding fault with a man for pillaging the diction-
ary. He mixed himself with whatever he took —
an incalculable increment. In the editions of his
poems, the thin line of text stands at the top of
the page like cream, and below it is the skim-milk
drawn from many milky mothers of the herd out
of which it has risen. But the thing to be considered is that, no matter where the material came
from, the result is Gray's own. Whether original
or not, he knew how to make a poem, a very rare
knowledge among men. The thought in Gray is
neither uncommon nor profound, and you may call
it beatified commonplace if you choose. I shall not
contradict you. I have lived long enough to know
that there is a vast deal of commonplace in the
world of no particular use to anybody, and am
thankful to the man who has the divine gift to
idealize it for me. Nor am I offended with this
odor of the library that hangs about Gray, for it
recalls none but delightful associations. It was in
the very best literature that Gray was steeped, and
I am glad that both he and we should profit by it.
If he appropriated a fine phrase wherever he found
it, it was by right of eminent domain, for surely
he was one of the masters of language. His praise
is that what he touched was idealized, and kindled

with some virtue that was not there before, but came from him.

And he was the most conscientious of artists. Some of the verses which he discards in deference to this conscientiousness of form which sacrifices the poet to the poem, the parts to the whole, and regards nothing but the effect to be produced, would have made the fortune of another poet. Take for example this stanza omitted from the " Elegy " (just before the Epitaph), because, says Mason, " he thought it was too long a parenthesis in this place."

> " There scattered oft, the earliest of the year,
>   By hands unseen are showers of violets found;
>   The redbreast loves to build and warble there,
>   And little footsteps lightly print the ground."

Gray might run his pen through this, but he could not obliterate it from the memory of men. Surely Wordsworth himself never achieved a simplicity of language so pathetic in suggestion, so musical in movement as this.

Any slave of the mine may find the rough gem, but it is the cutting and polishing that reveal its heart of fire; it is the setting that makes of it a jewel to hang at the ear of Time. If Gray cull his words and phrases here, there, and everywhere, it is he who charges them with the imaginative or picturesque touch which only he could give and which makes them magnetic. For example, in these two verses of " The Bard : " —

> " Amazement in his van with Flight combined,
>   And Sorrow's faded form and Solitude behind ! "

The suggestion (we are informed by the notes) came from Cowper and Oldham, and the amazement *combined* with flight sticks fast in prose. But the personification of Sorrow and the fine generalization of Solitude in the last verse which gives an imaginative reach to the whole passage are Gray's own. The owners of what Gray "conveyed" would have found it hard to identify their property and prove title to it after it had once suffered the Gray-change by steeping in his mind and memory.

When the example in our Latin Grammar tells us that *Mors communis est omnibus*, it states a truism of considerable interest, indeed, to the person in whose particular case it is to be illustrated, but neither new nor startling. No one would think of citing it, whether to produce conviction or to heighten discourse. Yet mankind are agreed in finding something more poignant in the same reflection when Horace tells us that the palace as well as the hovel shudders at the indiscriminating foot of Death. Here is something more than the dry statement of a truism. The difference between the two is that between a lower and a higher; it is, in short, the difference between prose and poetry. The oyster has begun, at least, to secrete its pearl, something identical with its shell in substance, but in sentiment and association how unlike! Malherbe takes the same image and makes it a little more picturesque, though, at the same time, I fear, a little more Parisian, too, when he says that the sentinel pacing before the gate of the Louvre cannot forbid Death an entrance to the King. And how

long had not that comparison between the rose's
life and that of the maiden dying untimely been a
commonplace when the same Malherbe made it ir-
reclaimably his own by mere felicity of phrase ? We
do not ask where people got their hints, but what
they made out of them. The commonplace is unhappily within reach of us all, and unhappily, too,
they are rare who can give it novelty and even
invest it with a kind of grandeur as Gray knew how
to do. If his poetry be a mosaic, the design is
always his own. He, if any, had certainly " the
last and greatest art," the art to please. Shall we
call everything mediocre that is not great ? Shall
we deny ourselves to the charm of sentiment because
we prefer the electric shudder that imagination
gives us ? Even were Gray's claims to being a
great poet rejected, he can never be classed with
the many, so great and uniform are the efficacy
of his phrase and the music to which he sets it.
This unique distinction, at least, may be claimed for
him without dispute, that he is the one English poet
who has written less and pleased more than any
other. Above all it is as a teacher of the art of
writing that he is to be valued. If there be any
well of English undefiled, it is to be found in him
and his master, Dryden. They are still standards
of what may be called classical English, neither
archaic nor modern, and as far removed from
pedantry as from vulgarity. They were

> " Tous deux disciples d'une escole
>   Où l'on forcene doucement,"

a school in which have been enrolled the **Great
Masters** of literature.

SOME LETTERS OF WALTER SAVAGE LANDOR.[1]

1888.

I was first directed to Landor's works by hearing how much store Emerson set by them. I grew
acquainted with them fifty years ago in one of those
arched alcoves in the old college library in Harvard
Hall, which so pleasantly secluded without wholly
isolating the student. That footsteps should pass
across the mouth of his Aladdin's Cave, or even
enter it in search of treasure, so far from disturbing only deepened his sense of possession. These
faint rumors of the world he had left served but
as a pleasant reminder that he was the privileged
denizen of another, beyond "the flaming bounds
of place and time." There, with my book lying at
ease and in the expansion of intimacy on the broad
window-shelf, shifting my cell from north to south
with the season, I made friendships, that have
lasted me for life, with Dodsley's "Old Plays,"
with Cotton's "Montaigne," with Hakluyt's "Voy-
ages," among others that were not in my father's
library. It was the merest browsing, no doubt, as
Johnson called it, but how delightful it was! All

[1] Written to introduce Landor's letters to the readers of *The
Century Magazine*, in which they were first published.

the more, I fear, because it added the stolen sweetness of truancy to that of study, for I should have
been buckling to my allotted task of the day.   I
do not regret that diversion of time to other than
legitimate expenses, yet shall I not gravely warn
my grandsons to beware of doing the like?

I was far from understanding all I heard in this
society of my elders into which I had smuggled myself, and perhaps it was as well for me; but those
who formed it condescended to me at odd moments
with the tolerant complacency of greatness, and
I did not go empty away.   Landor was in many
ways beyond me, but I loved the company he
brought, making persons for me of what before had
been futile names, and letting me hear the discourse
of men about whom Plutarch had so often told me
such delightful stories.   He charmed me, sometimes perhaps he imposed on me, with the stately
eloquence that moved to measure always, often to
music, and never enfeebled itself by undue emphasis, or raised its tone above the level of good breeding.   In those ebullient years of my adolescence
it was a wholesome sedative.   His sententiousness,
too, had its charm, equally persuasive in the carefully draped folds of the chlamys or the succinct
tunic of epigram.   If Plato had written in English,
I thought, it is thus that he would have written.
Here was a man, who knew what literature was,
who had assimilated what was best in it, and himself produced or reproduced it.

Three years later, while I was trying to persuade

myself that I was reading law, a friend [1] who knew
better gave me the first series of the "Imaginary
Conversations," in three volumes, to which I presently added the second series, and by degrees all
Landor's other books as I could pick them up, or
as they were successively published. Thus I grew
intimate with him, and, as my own judgment gradually affirmed itself, was driven to some abatement
of my hitherto unqualified admiration. I began
to be not quite sure whether the balance of his
sentences, each so admirable by itself, did not grow
wearisome in continuous reading, — whether it did
not hamper his freedom of movement, as when a
man poises a pole upon his chin. Surely he has
not the swinging stride of Dryden, which could
slacken to a lounge at will, nor the impassioned
rush of Burke. Here was something of that cadenced stalk which is the attribute of theatrical
kings. And sometimes did not his thunders also
remind us of the property-room? Though the

---

[1] Let me please myself by laying a sprig of rosemary ("that's
for remembrance ") on his grave. This friend was John Francis
Heath, of Virginia, who took his degree in 1840. He was the
handsomest man I have ever seen, and in every manly exercise
the most accomplished. His body was as exquisitely moulded as
his face was beautiful. I seem to see him now taking that famous
standing-jump of his, the brown curls blowing backward, or laying his hand on his horse's neck and vaulting into the saddle.
After leaving college he went to Germany and dreamed away nine
years at Heidelberg. We used to call him Hamlet, he could have
done so much and did so absolutely nothing. He died in the Con-
federate service, in 1862. He was a good swordsman (we used to
fence in those days), and the rumor of his German duels and of
his intimacy with Prussian princes reached us when some fellow-
student came home.

flash failed, did the long reverberation ever forget
to follow? But there is always something over-
passionate in the recoil of the young man from
the idols of the boy. Even now when I am more
temperate, however, I cannot help feeling that his
humor is horse-play; that he is often trivial and
not seldom slow; that he now and again misses the
true mean that can be grave without heaviness and
light without levity, though he would have dilated
on that virtue of our composite tongue which enabled it to make the distinction, and would have believed himself the first to discover it. He cannot
be familiar unless at the cost of his own dignity and
our respect. I sometimes question whether even
that quality in him which we cannot but recognize
and admire, his loftiness of mind, should not sometimes rather be called uppishness, so often is the
one caricatured into the other by a blusterous self-
confidence and self-assertion.

He says of himself, —

"Nature I loved, and, next to Nature, Art;"

but I am inclined to think that it was Art he loved
most. His perennial and abiding happiness was
in composition, in fitting word to word, and these
into periods, like a master-workman in mosaic.
This, perhaps, is why he preferred writing Latin
verse, because in doing that the joy of composing
was a more conscious joy. Certainly we miss in
him that quality of spontaneousness, that element
of luck, which so delights us in some of the lesser
and all the greater poets. By his own account

the most audacious of men, his thought and phrase
have seldom the happy audacity of what Montaigne
calls the first jump. Father Thames could never
have come upon *his* stage with both his banks on
the same side, refreshing as that innovation might
have been to an audience familiar with the hum-
drum habits of the river. Yet he is often content
to think himself original when he has lashed himself into extravagance; and the reserve of his better style is the more remarkable that he made
spoiled children of all his defects of character. It
might almost seem that he sought and found an
equipoise for his hasty violence of conduct in the
artistic equanimity of his literary manner. I think
he had little dramatic faculty. The creations of
his brain do not detach themselves from it and
become objective. He lived almost wholly in his
own mind and in a world of his own making which
his imagination peopled with casts after the antique.

His "Conversations" were imaginary in a truer
sense than he intended, for it is images rather than
persons that converse with each other in them.
Pericles and Phocion speak as we might fancy their
statues to speak, — nobly indeed, but with the cold
nobleness of marble. He had fire enough in himself, but his pen seems to have been a non-conduc-
tor between it and his personages. So little could
he conceive the real world as something outside
him, that nobody but himself was astonished when
he was cast in damages at the suit of a lady to
whom he had addressed verses that would have
blackened Canidia. But he had done it merely as

an exercise in verse; it was of that he was thinking, more than of her, and I doubt if she was so
near his consciousness, or so actual to him, as the
vile creatures of ancient Rome whose vices and
crimes he laid at her door. Even his in every
way admirable apothegms seem to be made out of
the substance of his mind, and not of his experience
or observation. And yet, with all his remoteness,
I can think of no author who has oftener brimmed
my eyes with tears of admiration or sympathy.

When we have made all deductions, he remains
great and, above all, individual. There is nothing
in him at second-hand. The least wise of men, he
has uttered through the mask of his interlocutors
(if I cannot trust myself to call them characters)
more wisdom on such topics of life and thought as
interested or occurred to him than is to be found
outside of Shakespeare; and that in an English
so pure, so harmonious, and so stirringly sonorous
that he might almost seem to have added new stops
to the organ which Milton found sufficient for his
needs. Though not a critic in the larger sense, —
he was too rash for that, too much at the mercy of
his own talent for epigram and seemingly conclusive
statement, — no man has said better things about
books than he. So well said are they, indeed, that
it seems ungrateful to ask if they are always just.
One would scruple to call him a great thinker, yet
surely he was a man who had great thoughts, and
when he was in the right mood these seam the ample heaven of his discourse like meteoric showers.
He was hardly a great poet, yet he has written

some of the most simply and conclusively perfect
lines that our own or any other language can show.
They float stately as swans on the tamer level of
his ordinary verse. Some of his shorter poems are
perfect as crystals. His metaphors are nobly original; they stand out in their bare grandeur like
statues against a background of sky; his similes
are fresh, and from nature; he plucks them as he
goes, like wild-flowers, nor interrupts his talk.
An intellectual likeness between him and Ben Jonson constantly suggests itself to me. Both had
burly minds with much apparent coarseness of fibre,
yet with singular delicacy of temperament.

In politics he was generally extravagant, yet so
long ago as 1812 he was wise enough (in a letter to
Southey) to call war between England and America
civil war, though he would not have been himself if
he had not added, "I detest the Americans as much
as you do." In 1826 he proposed a plan that
would have pacified Ireland and saved England
sixty years of odious mistake.

Ten or twelve years ago I tried to condense my
judgment of him into a pair of quatrains, written
in a copy of his works given to a dear young friend
on her marriage. As they were written in a happier mood than is habitual with me now, I may be
pardoned for citing them here with her permission,
and through her kindness in sending me a copy: —

"A villa fair, with many a devious walk
    Darkened with deathless laurels from the sun,
    Ample for troops of friends in mutual talk,
    Green Chartreuse for the reverie of one :
    Fixed here in marble, Rome and Athens gleam ;

Here is Arcadia, here Elysium too;
Anon an English voice disturbs our dream,
And Landor's self can Landor's spell undo.''

His books, as I seem to have hinted here, are
especially good for reading aloud in fitly sifted
company, and I am sure that so often as the experiment is tried this company will say, with Fran-
cesca : —

" Per più fïate gli occhi ci sospinse
Quella lettura, e scolorocci il viso.''

Landor was fond of saying that he should sup late,
but that the hall would be well lighted, and the
company, if few, of the choicest.   The table, indeed, has been long spread, but will he sit down till
the number of the guests is in nearer proportion to
that of the covers?   It is now forty years since the
collected edition of his works was published, probably, as was usual in his case, a small one.   Only
one re-impression has yet been called for.   Mr.
Forster's biography of him is a long plea for a new
trial.   It is a strange fate for a man who has written so much to interest, to instruct, to delight, and
to inspire his fellow-men.   Perhaps it is useless to
seek any other solution of the riddle than the old
habent sua fata libelli.   But I envy the man who
has before him the reading of those books for the
first time.   He will have a sensation as profound
as that of the peasant who wandered in to where
Kaiser Rothbart sits stately with his knights in the
mountain cavern biding his appointed time.

I saw Landor but once — when I went down from
London, by his invitation, to spend a day with him

at Bath in the late summer of 1852. His friend,
the late Mr. Kenyon, went with me, — his friend
and that of whoever deserved or needed friendship,
the divinely appointed *amicus curiæ* of mankind in
general.   For me it was and is a memorable day,
for Landor was to me an ancient, and it seemed
a meeting in Elysium.   I had looked forward to
it, nevertheless, with a twinge of doubt, for three
years before I had written a review of the new
edition of his works, in which I had discriminated
more than had been altogether pleasing to him.
But a guest was as sacred to Landor as to an Arab,
and the unaffected heartiness of his greeting at
once reassured me.   I have little to tell of our few
hours' converse, for the stream of memory, when
it has been flowing so long as mine, gathers an
ooze in its bed like that of Lethe, and in this the
weightier things embed themselves past recovery,
while the lighter, lying nearer the surface, may be
fished up again.   What I can recollect, therefore,
illustrates rather the manner of the man than his
matter.   His personal appearance has been sufficiently described by others.   I will only add, that
the suffused and uniform ruddiness of his face, in
which the forehead, already heightened by baldness,
shared, and something in the bearing of his head,
reminded me vividly of the late President Quincy,
as did also a certain hearty resonance of speech.
You felt yourself in the presence of one who was
emphatically a Man, not the image of a man; so
emphatically, indeed, that even Carlyle thought
the journey to Bath not too dear a price to pay for

seeing him, and found something royal in him. When I saw him he was in his seventy-eighth year, but erect and vigorous as in middle life. There was something of challenge even in the alertness of his pose, and the head was often thrown back like that of a boxer who awaits a blow. He had the air of the arena. I do not remember that his head was large, or his eyes in any way remarkable.

After the first greetings were over, I thought it might please him to know that I had made a pilgrimage to his Fiesolan villa. I spoke of the beauty of its site. I could not have been more clumsy, had I tried. "Yes," he almost screamed, "and I might have been there now, but for that in-tol-e-rrr-a-ble woman!" pausing on each syllable of the adjective as one who would leave an imprecation there, and making the *r* grate as if it were grinding its teeth at the disabilities which distance imposes on resentment. I was a little embarrassed by this sudden confidence, which I should not here betray had not Mr. Forster already laid Landor's domestic relations sufficiently bare. I am not sure whether he told me the story of his throwing his cook out of a window of this villa. I think he did, but it may have been Mr. Kenyon who told it me on the way back to London. The legend was, that after he had performed this summary act of justice, Mrs. Landor remonstrated with a "There, Walter! I always told you that one day you would do something to be sorry for in these furies of yours." Few men can be serene under an "I always told you so"—least of all men could Landor.

But he saw that here was an occasion where calm is more effective than tempest, and where a soft answer is more provoking than a hard. So he replied mildly: "Well, my dear, I *am* sorry, if that will do you any good. If I had remembered that our best tulip-bed was under that window, I 'd have flung the dog out of t' other."

He spoke with his wonted extravagance (he was always in extremes) of Prince Louis Napoleon: "I have seen all the great men that have appeared in Europe during the last half-century, and he is the ablest of them all. Had his uncle had but a tithe of his ability, he would never have died at St. Helena. The last time I saw the Prince before he went over to France, he said to me, 'Good-bye, Mr. Landor; I go to a dungeon or a throne.' 'Good-bye, Prince,' I answered. 'If you go to a dungeon, you may see me again; if to a throne, never!'" He told me a long story of some Merino sheep that had been sent him from Spain, and which George III. had "stolen." He seemed to imply that this was a greater crime than throwing away the American colonies, and a perfidy of which only kings could be capable. I confess that I thought the sheep as shadowy as those of Hans in Luck, for I was not long in discovering that Landor's memory had a great deal of imagination mixed with it, especially when the subject was anything that related to himself. It was not a memory, however, that was malignly treacherous to others.

I mentioned his brother Robert's " Fountain of

Arethusa;" told him how much it had interested
me, and how particularly I had been struck with
the family likeness to himself in it. He assented;
said it *was* family likeness, not imitation, and
added: "Yes, when it came out many people, even
some of my friends, thought it was mine, and told
me so. My answer always was, 'I wish to God I
could have written it!'" He spoke of it with un-
feigned enthusiasm, though then, I believe, he was
not on speaking terms with his brother. Whenever, indeed, his talk turned, as it often would, to
the books or men he liked, it rose to a passionate
appreciation of them. Even upon indifferent matters he commonly spoke with heat, as if he had
been contradicted, or hoped he might be. There
was no prophesying his weather by reading the
barometer of his face. Though the index might
point never so steadily to *Fair*, the storm might
burst at any moment. His quiet was that of the
cyclone's pivot, a conspiracy of whirlwind. Of
Wordsworth he spoke with a certain alienated respect, and made many abatements, not as if jeal-
ous, but somewhat in the mood of that Athenian
who helped ostracize Aristides. Of what he said I
recollect only something which he has since said
in print, but with less point. Its felicity stamped
it on my memory. "I once said to Mr. Wordsworth, 'One may mix as much poetry with prose
as one likes, it will exhilarate the whole; but the
moment one mixes a drop of prose with poetry, it
precipitates the whole.' He never forgave me!"
Then followed that ringing and reduplicated laugh
of his, so like the joyous bark of a dog when he

starts for a ramble with his master. Of course he
did not fail to mention that exquisite sea-shell
which Wordsworth had conveyed from *Gebir* to
ornament his own mantelpiece.

After lunch, he led us into a room the whole
available wall-space of which was hung with pictures, nearly all early Italian. As I was already
a lover of Botticelli, I think I may trust the judgment I then inwardly pronounced upon them, that
they were nearly all aggressively bad. They were
small, so that the offence of each was trifling, but
in the aggregate they were hard to bear. I waited
doggedly to hear him begin his celebration of them,
dumfounded between my moral obligation to be as
truthful as I dishonestly could and my social duty
not to give offence to my host. However, I was
soon partially relieved. The picture he wished
to show was the head of a man, an ancestor, he told
me, whose style of hair and falling collar were of
the second quarter of the seventeenth century.
Turning sharply on me, he asked: "Does it remind you of anybody?" Of course this was a simple riddle; so, after a diplomatic pause of deliberation, I replied, cheerfully enough : "I think I see
a likeness to you in it." There was an appreciable
amount of fib in this, but I trust it may be pardoned me as under duress. "Right!" he exploded,
with the condensed emphasis of a rifle. "Does it
remind you of anybody else?" For an instant I
thought my retribution had overtaken me, but in a
flash of inspiration I asked myself, "Whom would
Landor like best to resemble?" The answer was
easy, and I gave it forthwith : "I think I see a

likeness to Milton." "Right again!" he cried triumphantly. "It *does* look like me, and it *does* look like Milton. That is the portrait of my ancestor, Walter Noble, Speaker of one of Charles First's parliaments. I was showing this portrait one day to a friend, when he said to me, 'Landor, how can you pride yourself on your descent from this sturdy old cavalier — you who would have cut off Charles's head with the worst of 'em?' '*I* cut off his head? Never!' 'You wouldn't? I'm astonished to hear you say that. What would you have done with him?' 'What would I have done? Why, *hanged* him, like any other malefactor!'" This he trumpeted with such a blare of victory as almost made his progenitor rattle on the wall where he hung. Whether the portrait was that of an ancestor, or whether he had bought it as one suitable for his story, I cannot say. If an ancestor, it could only have been Michael (not Walter) Noble, Member of Parliament (not Speaker) during the Civil War, and siding with the Commons against the King. Landor had confounded him with Sir Arnold Savage (a Speaker in Henry Seventh's time), whom he had adopted as an ancestor, though there was no probable, certainly no provable, community of blood between them. This makes the anecdote only the more characteristic as an illustration of the freaks of his innocently fantastic and creative memory. I could almost wish my own had the same happy faculty, when I see how little it has preserved of my conversation, so largely monologue on his part, with a man so memorable.

1889.

BIOGRAPHY in these communicative days has become so voluminous that it might seem calculated
rather for the ninefold vitality of another domestic
animal than for the less lavish allotment of man.
Only such renewed leases of life could justify the
writing or suffice for the reading of these too often
supererogatory confidences. Only a man like the
great Julius, who new-moulded the world and
stamped his effigy on the coinage of political
thought still current, has a right to so much of our
curiosity as we are now expected to put at the service of an average general or bishop. "Nothing
human is foreign to me" was said long ago, chiefly
by the Latin Grammar, and has been received as
the pit and gallery receive a moral sentiment which
does not inconvenience themselves, but which they
think likely to give the boxes an uneasy qualm.
But biography has found out a process by which
what is human may be so thrust upon us as to become
*in*human, and one is often tempted to wish that a
great deal of it might not only be made foreign to

[1] This paper was originally printed as an introduction to an edition of Walton's *Angler*, edited by Mr. John Bartlett, and published in 1889 by Messrs. Little, Brown & Co., through whose cour-
tesy it is included in this collection.

us, but firmly kept so. Plutarch, a man of the
most many-sided moral and intellectual interests,
had a truer sense of proportion, and tempers his
amiable discursiveness with an eye to his neighbor's dial.   And in his case the very names of
his heroes are mostly so trumpet-like as both to
waken attention and to warrant it, ushering in the
bearers of them like that *flourish* on the Elizabethan stage which told that a king was coming.
How should Brown or Smith or any other dingy
monosyllable of Saxon indistinction compete for
conjuration with Pelopidas or Timoleon?   Even
within living memory Napoleon had a prodigious
purchase in his name alone, and prettily confirmed
the theory of Mr. Shandy.

The modern biographer has become so indiscrim-
inate, so unconscious of the relative importance of
a single life to the Universe, so careless of the just
limits whether of human interest or endurance, so
communistic in assuming that all men are entitled
to an equal share of what little time there is left
in the world, that many a worthy, whom a para-
graph from the right pen might have immmortal-
ized, is suffocated in the trackless swamps of two
octavos.   Meditating over these grievances with
the near prospect of a biography to write, I am
inclined to apply what was said of States to men
also, and call him happiest who has left fewest ma-
terials for history.   It is at least doubtful whether
gossip gain body by bottling.   In these chattering
days when nobody who really *is* nobody can stir
forth without the volunteer accompaniment of a

brass band, when there is a certificated eye at every
keyhole, and when the Public Informer has become
so essential a minister to the general comfort that
the world cannot go about its business of a morning
till its intellectual appetite is appeased with the
latest doings and sayings of John Doe and Richard
Roe, there is healing in the gentlemanlike reserves
of the past, a benign sense of seclusion, a comfort
such as loved hands bring to fevered brows, in the
thought of one who, like Walton, has been safe
for two hundred years in the impregnable strong-
hold of the grave. Malice domestic, treason, in-
terviews, nothing can touch him further. The
sanctities of *his* life, at least, cannot be hawked
about the streets or capitalized in posters as a whet
to the latest edition of the Peeping Tom. If it be
the triumph of an historian to make the great high-
ways of the olden time populous and noisy, or even
vulgar, with their old life again, it is nevertheless
a consolation that we may still find by-paths there,
dumb as those through a pine forest, sacred to
meditation and to grateful thoughts.

Such a by-path is the life of Walton. Though
it lead us through nearly a hundred years of history, many of them stormy with civil or anxious
with foreign war, the clamor of events is seldom
importunate, and the petulant drums are muffled
with a dreamy remoteness. So far as he himself
could shape its course, it leads us under the shadow
of honeysuckle hedges, or along the rushy banks of
silence-loving streams, or through the claustral hush
of cathedral closes, or where the shadow of the vil-

lage church-tower creeps round its dial of green graves below, or to the company of thoughtful and godly men. He realized the maxim which Voltaire preached, but so assiduously avoided practising, — *bene vixit qui bene latuit.* He did his best to fulfil the apostle's injunction in studying to be quiet. Whether such fugitive and cloistered virtue as his come within the sweep of Milton's gravely cadenced lash or not, whether a man do not owe himself more to the distasteful publicity of active citizenship than to the petting of his own private tastes or talents, as Walton thought it right and found it sweet to do, may be a question. There can be none that the contemplation of such a life both soothes and charms, and we sigh to think that the like of it is possible no longer. Where now would the fugitive from the espials of our modern life find a sanctuary which telegraph or telephone had not deflowered? I do not mean that Walton was an idle man, who, as time was given him for nothing, thought that he might part with it for nothing too. If he had been, I should not be writing this. He left behind him two books, each a masterpiece in its own simple and sincere way, and only the contemplative leisure of a life like his could have secreted the precious qualities that assure them against decay.

But Walton's life touches the imagination at more points than this of its quietude and inwardness. It opens many windows to the fancy. Its opportunities were as remarkable as its length. Twenty-two years old when Shakespeare died, he lived long enough to have read Dryden's "Absalom and

Achitophel." He had known Ben Jonson and
Chillingworth and Drayton and Fuller; he had
exchanged gossip with Antony à Wood; he was
the friend of Donne and Wotton and King; he
had seen George Herbert; and how many more
sons of Memory must he not have known or seen
in all those years so populous with men justly
famous! Of the outward husk of this life of his we
know comfortably little, but of the kernel much,
and that chiefly from such unconscious glimpses as
he himself has given us.

Isaac, or (as he preferred to spell the name)
Izaak, Walton was born at Stafford, on the 9th of
August, 1593, of a family in the rank of substantial yeomen long established in Staffordshire. Of
his mother not even the name is known, and of his
father we know only that his baptismal name was
Jervis, and that he was buried on the 11th of Feb-
ruary, 1596–97. Surely the short and simple
annals of the poor have been seldom more laconic
than this. Sir Harris Nicolas, author of the first
trustworthy Life of Walton, yielding for once to
the biographer's weakness for appearances, says
that he "received a good, though not, strictly
speaking, classical education." Considering that
absolutely nothing is known of Walton's schooling,
the concession to historical conscientiousness made
in the parenthetic "strictly speaking" is amusing.
We have the witness of documents in Walton's
own handwriting that he could never have been
taught even the rudiments of Latin; for he spells
the third person singular of the perfect tense of

obire, obiet, separate, seperate, and *divided, devided.* And these documents are printed by Sir Harris himself. After this one finds it hard to conceive what a classical education, loosely speaking, would be. In the list of Walton's books there is none that is not in English. It is enough for us that he contrived to pick up somewhere and somehow a competent mastery of his mother-tongue (far harder because seeming easier than Latin), and a diction of persuasive simplicity, capable of dignity where that was natural and becoming, such as not even the universities can bestow.

It is not known in what year he went to London. It has been conjectured, and with much probability, that he was sent thither to serve his apprenticeship with a relative, Henry Walton, a haberdasher. Of this Henry Walton nothing is known beyond what we are told by his will, and this shows us that he had connections with Staffordshire. That Izaak Walton gave the name of Henry to two sons in succession seems to show some kind of close relation between them and some earlier Henry. But Mr. Nicholls discovered in the records of the Ironmongers' Company for 1617–18 the following entry: "Isaac Walton was made one of the Ironmongers' Company by Thomas Grinsell, citizen and ironmonger." That Walton had relatives of this name appears from a legacy in his will to the widow of his "Cosen Grinsell." On the whole, whatever light is let in by this chink serves only to make the abundant darkness more visible. May there not have been another Isaac, perhaps a cousin, to dis-

tinguish himself from whom ours gave to his sur-
name its fantastic spelling? What is certain is
that he was already in London in 1619. In that
year was published the second edition of a poem,
"The Love of Amos and Laura," which, to judge
by all that I know of it, the dedication, must happily have been very soon gathered to its fathers;
but it has two points of interest. It is dedicated
to Walton by a certain S. P., who may have been
the Samuel Purchas of the "Pilgrims;" and in this
dedication there are expressions which show that
Walton's character was already, in his twenty-
sixth year, marked by the same attractiveness and
purity and the same aptness for friendship which
endeared him in later life to so many good and eminent men. S. P., after calling him his "more
than thrice-beloved friend," tells him that he is
the cause that the poem "is now as it is," and that
it might have been called his had it been better,
but that "No ill thing can be clothed with thy
verse." We should infer that Walton had done
much in the way of revision, and not only this, but
that he was already known, among his friends at
least, as a writer of verse himself. It is puzzling,
however, that the first edition was published in
1613, when Walton was barely twenty, and that
the second differs from the first in a single word
only. In the only known copy of this earlier edition (which, to be sure, is otherwise imperfect) the
dedication is not to be found. Sir Harris Nicolas
suggests that Walton may have revised the poem in
manuscript, but it seems altogether unlikely that he

should have been called in as a consulting physician at so early an age. More than twenty years later, in the preface to his Life of Donne, he speaks of his "artless pencil," and several times elsewhere alludes to his literary inadequacy. But this deprecation may have been merely a shiver of his habitual modesty, or, as is more likely, a device of his literary adroitness. He certainly must have had considerable practice in the making of verse before he wrote his Elegy on Donne (1633), his first published essay in authorship. The versification of this, if sometimes rather stiff, is for the most part firm and not inharmonious. It is easier in its gait than that of Donne in his Satires, and shows the manly influence of Jonson.

Walton, at any rate, in course of time, attained, at least in prose, to something which, if it may not be called style, was a very charming way of writing, all the more so that he has an innocent air of not knowing how it is done. Natural endowment and predisposition may count for nine in ten of the chances of success in this competition; but no man ever achieved, as Walton sometimes did, a simplicity which leaves criticism helpless, by the mere light of nature alone. Nor am I speaking without book. In his Life of Herbert he prints a poem of Donne's addressed to Herbert's mother, in which there is allusion to certain hymns. Walton adds a few words which seem to follow each other with as little forethought as the notes of a thrush's song: "These hymns are now lost to us, but doubtless they were such as they two now sing in Heaven." Now on the inside cover of his Eusebius Walton has written three attempts at this sentence, each of them very far from the concise beauty to which he at last constrained himself. Simplicity, when it is not a careless gift of the Muse, is the last and most painful achievement of conscientious self-denial. He seems also to have had the true literary memory, which stores up the apt or pleasing word for use on occasion. I have noticed more than one instance of it, but one must suffice. In Donne's beautiful poem, "A Valediction Forbidding Mourning," is this stanza :—

> " Dull sublunary lovers' love,
>   Whose soul is sense, cannot admit
>   Absence, because that doth remove
>   Those things that elemented it."

Walton felt the efficacy of the word "elemented," and laid it by for employment at the first vacancy. I find it more than once in his writings.

Of the personal history of Walton during his life in London we know very little more than that he was living in Fleet Street in 1624, that from 1628 to 1644 he lived in Chancery Lane, and that he was twice married. Perhaps the most important event during all these years in its value to his mind and character was his making the acquaintance of Donne, to whose preaching he was a sedulous listener. This acquaintance became a friendship by which he profited till Donne's death in 1631. There needs no further witness to his intelligence or to his worth.

Walton's first wife, to whom he was married in 1624, was Rachel Floud, daughter of Susannah Cranmer, who was the daughter of Thomas, grand-nephew of the martyr. By her, who died in 1640, he had six sons and one daughter, all of whom died in infancy or early childhood. Six years after his first wife's death Walton married Anne Ken, a sister by the half blood of Bishop Ken. Of this marriage there were three children, — one son, Izaak, who lived but a short time; a daughter Anne; and another Izaak, who survived his father, and died in 1719, a canon of Salisbury.

In the third edition of "The Complete Angler" (1664) appear for the first time some verses by Walton called "The Angler's Wish." Among other blisses is mentioned that of hearing "my Chlora sing a song." In the fifth edition (1676) "Kenna" is substituted for "Chlora," and the reference to Walton's second wife is obvious. It has been supposed that "Chlora" was an imperfect anagram for "Rachel;" and that Walton, like some better poets, Poe notably, had economized his inspiration by serving up the same verses cold to a second or even third mistress; but he was incapable of such amatory double-dealing. Sir Harris Nicolas, by calling attention to the dates, at least makes it very unlikely that he was guilty of it. The verses were first published twenty years after the death of his first wife, and the name "Kenna" does not appear till his second had been fourteen years in her grave. Sir Harris failed to remark that Walton uses "Chlora" as the name of a shepherdess in an eclogue on the restoration of Charles II. Confronted with this fact, the supposed anagram turns out to be a mare's-nest, like the "Lutero" Rossetti found in Dante's "Veltro." Anne Walton herself died in 1662.

There is no certainty as to what Walton's occupation may have been further than that he was a tradesman of some sort, and probably, since he was thirty years in amassing the modest competence that sufficed him, in a small way. Whether large or small is of little interest to us, for his real business in this world was to write the Lives and "The Complete Angler," and to leave the example of a useful and unspotted life behind him. But it is amusing to find Mr. Major, with that West-End view of the realities of life which Englishmen of a certain class feel it proper to take, arguing that Walton's business must have been of a wholesale character because the place in which it was carried on was cramped, and moreover shared by a certain John Mason, hosier. One is irresistibly tempted to parody the notorious verse, and say, —

"His trade was great because his shop was small."

"What room would there have been for the display of goods?" asks Mr. Major, with triumphant conviction, forgetting that in those days the space for that purpose was found in the street. Walton's removal to Chancery Lane may imply an enlargement of business; and this, so far as it goes, must suffice to console whoever values a man not for what he is, but by the round of the social ladder on which he happens to be standing. If the humbleness of Walton's station helped him toward that unaffected modesty which is so gracious in him and so dignified, we may well be thankful for it.

Walton seems to have done his duty as a citizen with exemplary fidelity.   Between 1632 and 1644, when he moved out of the parish, the register of St. Dunstan's in the West shows him to have been successively scavenger (which Sir Harris Nicolas prudently deodorizes by calling it vaguely "a parish office"), juryman, constable, grand-juryman, overseer of the poor, and vestry-man, — enough, one might say, to satisfy any reasonable ambition for civic honors at a time when they meant honest work done for honest wages.

Walton's first appearance as an author was in an elegy, which, after the fashion of the day, accompanied the first edition of Donne's poems (1633).   This species of verse, whether in the writing or the reading, is generally the most dreary compulsory labor to which man can be doomed. The poet climbs the doleful treadmill without getting an inch the higher; and as we watch him we are wearied with the reality of a toil which seems to have no real object.   Once in my life I have heard a funeral elegy which was wholly adequate. It was the long quavering howl of a dog under a window of the chamber in which his master had at that moment died.   It was Nature's cry of grief and terror at first sight of Death.   That faithful creature was not trying to say something; so far from it, that even the little skill in articulation which his race has acquired was choked in the gripe

of such disaster. Consolation would shrink away
abashed from the presence of so helpless a grief.
With elegiac poets it is otherwise, for it is of themselves and of their verses that they are thinking.
They distil a precious cordial from their tears.
They console themselves by playing variations on
their inconsolability. Their triumphs are won over
our artistic sense, not over our human fellow-feeling.
Yet now and then in the far inferior verse of far
inferior men there will be some difficult word with
a sob in it that moves as no artifice can move, and
brings back to each of us his private loss with a
strange sense of comfort in feeling that somewhere,
no matter how far away in the past, there was one
who had suffered like ourselves and would not be
appeased by setting his pain to music. There is
something of this in Walton's Elegy on Donne. I
do not believe that he was thinking of his poetical
paces as he wrote it; or, if he was, he forgets them
from time to time and falls into his natural gait.
What he said ten years later in writing of Cart-
wright seems true of this, —

> " Muses, I need you not, for Grief and I
>   Can in your absence weave an elegy."

I should be yielding to my partiality for Walton
if I called these verses poetry; but there is at least,
in the eloquence of their honest sorrow, a tendency
to become so which stops little short of it. and
which is too often missed in the carefully cadenced
ululation of similar efforts. Here, indeed, there
seems no effort at all, and that surely is a crowning
mercy. There is one phrase whose laconic pathos

I find it hard to match elsewhere. It is where he bids his thoughts "forget he loved me." This is the true good breeding of sorrow. It may as well be said here, once for all, that Walton was no poet, so far as rhythm is an essential element of expression. His lyrics are mechanical and club-footed. He succeeded best in that measure, the rhymed couplet of ten syllables, which detaches it-self least irreconcilably from prose. The nearer an author comes to being a poet, so much the worse for him should he persist in making verse the in-terpreter of his thought; so much the better for him should he wisely abandon it for something closer to the habitual dialect of men. I think that Walton's prose owes much of its charm to the po-etic sentiment in him which was denied a refuge in verse, and that his practice in metres may have given to his happier periods a measure and a music they would otherwise have wanted. That he had this practice has a direct bearing on the question of the authorship of "Thealma and Clearchus," of which I must say something at the proper time. Walton had not the strong passions which poets break to the light harness of verse, and indeed they and longevity such as his are foaled by dams of very different race. But he loved poetry, and the poetry he loved was generally good. He had also some critical judgment in it. Speaking of Marlowe's "Come live with me," and Raleigh's answer to it, he says, "They were old-fashioned poetry, but choicely good; I think much better than the strong lines that are now in fashion in this critical age." His simplicity, it should seem, was not only a gift, but a choice as well.

Not long before the publication of a volume of Donne's sermons (1640), Walton wrote a life of the author, which was prefixed to them. This piety was not volunteered, but devolved on him by the death of their common friend, Sir Henry Wotton (December, 1639), for whom he had been collecting the material. Donne lost nothing, and the world gained much, by this substitution; for Walton thus learned by accident where his true talent lay, and was encouraged to write those other Lives which, with this, make the volume that has endeared him to all who choose that their souls should keep good company. In a preface, beautiful alike for its form and the sentiment embodied in it, after a pretty apology for his own deficiencies, he says, "But be this to the disadvantage of the person represented, certain I am it is to the advantage of the beholder who shall here see the author's [Donne] picture *in a natural dress*, which ought to beget faith in what is spoken." And not only that, but Walton's picture too! In this preference of the homely and familiar, and in an artlessness which is not quite so artless as it would fain appear, lies the charm that never stales of Walton's manner. He would have applied his friend Wotton's verse to himself, and affirmed "simple truth his utmost skill," but he was also a painstaking artist in his own way.

As illustrations, take this sentence from the Life of Donne, describing him after the death of his wife: —

"Thus, as the Israelites sat mourning by the rivers of Babylon when they remembered Zion, so he gave some ease to his oppressed heart by thus venting his sorrows; thus he began the day and ended the night; ended the restless night and began the weary day in lamentations."

Or this, of the nightingale, worthy to compete with Crashawe's, or with Jeremy Taylor's lark: —

"But the nightingale, another of my airy creatures, breathes such sweet loud music out of her little instrumental throat, that it might make mankind to think miracles are not ceased. He that at midnight, when the very laborer sleeps securely, should hear, as I have very often, the clear airs, the sweet descants, the natural rising and falling, the doubling and redoubling of her voice, might well be lifted above earth, and say, 'Lord, what music hast Thou provided for the saints in heaven, when Thou affordest bad men such music on earth?'"

He had learned of his great contemporaries also to turn and wind those many-membered periods which in unskilful hands become otherwise-minded as a herd of swine. The passage in the Introduction to his revised Life of Donne where he compares himself to Pompey's bondman, and that in the Preface to the Life of Herbert in which he speaks of Mary Magdalene, may serve as examples; and in these neither are the words caught at random, nor do they fall into those noble modulations by chance. And he could be succinct at need, as where he says: "He that praises Richard Hooker praises God, who hath given such gifts to men."

Walton tells us that he saw the Scotch Cove-

nanters, when in 1644 they "came marching with it
[the Covenant] gloriously upon their pikes and in
their hats. . . . This I saw and suffered by it."
whether in mind or purse he leaves doubtful. In
this year he ceased to be an inhabitant of the Parish
of St. Dunstan; and from that time till 1650,
when he took a house in Clerkenwell, he for the
most part vanishes. We know incidentally that
he was in London once in the course of the year
1645, and once again in that of 1647. But these
may have been flying visits, for there is no evidence
that his second marriage (1646) took place there;
and the statement of Antony à Wood, who knew
him well, makes it probable that he may have spent
at Stafford, where he had a small property, the
years during which he cannot be shown to have
lived anywhere else. To a man with his opinions,
London could not have been more amiable during
the Long Parliament and the Protectorate than
during the reign of Charles II. to a man of his
morals.

The solitude of Stafford, where, to cite his own
words, he could

    " Linger long days by Swaynham brook,"

seems more suitable to the conception and gestation
of such a book as "The Complete Angler" than
London could have been to a man whose companionable instincts were so strong that even fishing was not perfect happiness without a friend to
share it.

That the "Angler" was begun some years be-

fore it was published is rendered more probable
by Walton's saying of Marlowe's song which he
quotes, that it "was made at least fifty years ago."
He was likely to know something about Marlowe
through his own friendship with Drayton, who was
the first adequately to signalize the poet's merit.
Marlowe died in 1593, and the "at least fifty
years" would bring us down to the Stafford period. There are passages in Walton which lead me
to think he may have spent abroad some part of
the time during which he is invisible to us. He
set great store by the advantages of foreign travel,
and gave his son the benefit of them.

It seems likely that he gave up business in 1644,
and it may have been at Stafford that he saw
some foraging party from Leslie's army which would
not have spared his uncovenanted chickens. Internal evidence makes it likely that in 1646 he wrote
the preface to Quarles's "Shepherd's Eclogues,"
and that he was on terms of friendly acquaintance
with him as a brother of the angle. He may have
borrowed the name "Clora" from Quarles. It is
true that he has put an *h* into it, but his spelling is
always according to his own lights (mostly will-o'-
the-wisps); and there are people who think crystals
less lustrous without that letter which may be picked
up anywhere in the land of Cokayne, where it
is dropped so often. In 1650 he published the
"Reliquiæ Wottonianæ," prefixing to them a life
of the author, printed in haste, he tells us, but cor-
rected in later editions. The "Angler" appeared
in 1653, and a second edition came out two years

later. It was while he was in London during this latter year, probably to correct his proof-sheets, that he met Sanderson. who was there to perform the same function for the preface to a volume of sermons. Walton's account of this meeting is so characteristic that I shall quote it: —

" About the time of his printing this excellent Preface, I met him accidentally in *London* in sad-colored clothes, and, God knows, far from being costly. The place of our meeting was near to *Little Britain*, where he had been to buy a book which he then had in his hand. We had no inclination to part presently, and therefore turned to stand in a corner under a pent-house, for it began to rain, and immediately the wind rose and the rain increased so much that both became so inconvenient as to force us into a cleanly house, where we had bread. cheese, ale, and a fire for our money. This rain and wind were so obliging to me as to force our stay there for at least an hour, to my great content and advantage. . . . And I gladly remember and mention it as an argument of my happiness and his great humility and condescension."

It is exactly as if he were telling us of it, and this sweet persuasiveness of the living and naturally cadenced voice is never wanting in Walton. It is indeed his distinction, and it is a very rare quality in writers, upon most of whom, if they ever happily forget themselves and fall into the tone of talk, the pen too soon comes sputtering in. The passage is interesting too because it illustrates both Walton's love of good company and his Boswellian sensitiveness to the attraction of superior men.

Much as he loved fishing, it was in the minds of
such men that he loved best to fish. And what
a memory was his! The place, the sad-colored
clothes, the book just bought, the rain and then
the wind, the pent-house, the tavern, the bread,
the ale, the fire, — everything is there that makes
a picture. Then he reports Sanderson's discourse;
and having done that, is reminded that this is a
good time to give us a description of his person.
In reading Walton's Lives (and no wonder Johnson
loved them so [1]) I have a feeling that I have met
him in the street and am hearing them from his
own lips. I ask him about Donne, let us say. He
begins, but catching sight of some one who passes,
gives me in parenthesis an account of him, comes
back to Donne, and keeps on with him till somebody else goes by about whom he has an anecdote
to tell; and so we get a leash of biographies in one.
It is very delightful, and though more rambling
than Plutarch, comes nearer to him than any other
life-writing I can think of. Indeed, I should be
inclined to say that Walton had a genius for rambling rather than that it was his foible. The comfortable feeling he gives us that we have a definite
purpose, mitigated with the license to forget it at
the first temptation and take it up again as if nothing had happened, thus satisfying at once the
conscientious and the natural man, is one of Walton's most prevailing charms. What vast bal-

[1] Gray must have loved them too, and his *Ode on a Distant
Prospect of Eton College* was suggested by a passage in the Life
of Wotton.

ances of leisure does he not put to our credit ! To
read him is to go a-fishing with all its bewitching
charms and contingencies. If there be many a dull
reach in the stream of his discourse, where contemplation might innocently lapse into slumber, it is
full also of nooks and eddies where nothing but our
own incompetence will balk us of landing a fine
fish. In this story of his meeting with Sanderson there is another point to be noticed. Walton's memory is always discreet, always well-bred.
It never blabs. I think that one little fact is
purposely omitted here, namely, who paid for the
good cheer at the tavern. The scot was paid, to
be sure, with "our money," but I doubt very much
whether the poor country parson's purse were the
lighter for it.

In 1658 Walton published separately the second
and revised edition of his Life of Donne, with a
preface engagingly full of himself. I say "engagingly full," because when he speaks of himself he
never seems to usurp on other people, but only to
share with all mankind a confidence to which they
had as good a right as he. In 1660 he prefixed a
congratulatory eclogue on the Restoration to a volume of Alexander Brome's Songs. In this he con-
trives to bring in the praise of his friend's verses,
and combines the tediousness of the Commendatory
and the Birthday styles with entire success. Never
inspired in verse, he becomes laborious unless
where his feelings are stirred to the roots, as in the
Elegy on Donne.

In 1662 he was at Worcester, the guest, proba-

bly, of his friend Bishop Morley. Here his second
wife died and lies buried in the cathedral, with an
inscription by him, simple and affectionate. In
that year he removed with Morley (on his translation) to Winchester, and there spent the rest of
his vigorous old age. From time to time he must
have visited Charles Cotton, whose father he had
known. We have no record of these visits (spent
in fishing) further than that one of them is spoken
of in a letter of Walton as proposed in 1676.
This was in his eighty-third year, and implies in
him that longevity of the taste for out-of-door
sports and of the muscle to endure their fatigues
which are almost peculiar to Englishmen. Cotton
was a Royalist country-gentleman with a handsome
estate, which, after sidling safely through the in-
tricacies of the Civil War, trickled pleasantly away
through the chinks of its master's profusion. He
was an excellent poet and a thorough master of
succulently idiomatic English, which he treated
with a country-gentlemanlike familiarity, as his
master, Montaigne, had treated French. The two
men loved one another, and this speaks well for
the social charity of both. There must have been
delicately understood and mutually respectful con-
ventions of silence in an intimacy between the pla-
cidly believing author of the Lives and the translator
of him who invented the Essay. Walton loved a
gentleman of blue blood as honestly as Johnson
did, and was, I am sure, as sturdily independent
withal. He could condone almost anything, that
had no taint of personal dishonor, in a gentleman

and a Cavalier. His nature was incapable of envy,
and, himself of obscurest lineage, there was nothing
he relished more keenly than the long pedigrees of
other people. While he enjoyed, he had also, I
fancy, not merely a sense of joint ownership, but
perhaps of something like over-lordship, as in that
winsome passage of the "Angler" he makes Venator say, after describing the landscape he has been
looking on: "As I thus sat joying in my own
happy condition and pitying the poor rich man that
owns this and many other pleasant groves and meadows about me, I did thankfully remember what my
Saviour said, that the meek possess the earth."
But with him the more noble the ancestry, the
worse for their degenerous representative. A pedigree had not the right flavor for Walton unless
newly spiced with achievement from generation
to generation. In his Life of Sanderson, after
proclaiming with heraldic satisfaction that he was
of ancient family, he blows this trumpet-blast
against the recreant: —

"For titles not acquired, but derived only, do but
show us who of our ancestors have and how they have
achieved that honor which their descendants claim and
may not be worthy to enjoy. For if those titles descend
to persons that degenerate into vice and break off the
continued line of learning or valor or that virtue that
acquired them. they destroy the very foundation upon
which that honor was built, and all the rubbish of their
vices ought to fall heavy on such dishonorable heads;
ought to fall so heavy as to degrade them of their titles
and blast their memories with reproach and shame."

It is plain that Walton, had he lived now, would have made short work with an unsavory Peer. It is noticeable too that he gives Learning precedence over Valor.

Walton had a genius for friendships and an amiability of nature ample for the comfortable housing of many at a time; he had even a special genius for bishops, and seems to have known nearly the whole Episcopal bench of his day; but his friendship, like Lamb's, did not slink away from a fortune out at elbows, and he had, I more than suspect, a curiosity hospitable enough to entertain a broken gentleman (like the Carey whom he speaks of having known) if he had good talk or narrative or honest mirth in him and producible on demand. His friend Alexander Brome was surely no precisian. But these less reputable intimates he made welcome in a back-parlor of his mind, away from the street and with the curtains drawn, as if he would fain hide them even from himself.[1] His habitual temper sought serious and thoughtful company, and he valued respectability as a wise man must, his own self-respect as a good man ought. But Cotton was a man of genius,[2] whose life was cleanlier than his Muse always cared to be. If he wrote the Virgil Travesty, he

---

[1] In his Life of Hooker, having to speak of George Sandys, he mentions his Travels, and his translations in verse from the Psalms and Job. He is silent about his version of Ovid's *Metamorphoses* (done in Virginia), though the book was in his own library.

[2] Not yet extinct among his descendants. The late Lady Marian Alford, besides her social talents, had every gift that Fortune bestows on the artist save that of poverty.

also wrote verses which the difficult Wordsworth
could praise, and a poem of gravely noble mood
addressed to Walton on his Lives, in which he
shows a knowledge of what goodness is that no bad
man could have acquired. Let one line of it at
least shine in my page, not as a sample but for
its own dear sake: —

> " For in a virtuous act all good men share."

Those must have been delightful evenings which
the two friends spent together after the day's fishing. Well into the night they must have lingered,
with much excellent discourse of books and men,
now serious, now playful, much personal anecdote
and reminiscence. Perhaps it was as well that
Dr. Morley should be at Winchester, with all respect be it said, and not forgetting that Walton
has told us he "loved such mirth as did not make
friends ashamed to look upon one another next
morning."

At Walton's request, Cotton wrote in ten days
the treatise on fly-fishing which was added to the
fifth edition of "The Complete Angler" in 1676.
What he says of Walton in it is interesting, and
the reverence he expresses for his character especially so as coming from a man of the world. "My
father Walton," he makes Piscator say, "will be
seen twice in no man's company he does not like,
and likes none but such as he believes to be very
honest men." It should be remembered that in
those days the word "honest" had to the initiated
ear a political and ecclesiastical as well as a moral

meaning. Cotton was a far better poet than Walton, and had a more practised hand; yet his supplement to the "Angler" wants that charm of inadvertency with which Walton knew how to make his most careful sentences waylay the ear, and his truly poetic sympathy with the sights and sounds of every-day Nature. Its chief value, I think, lies in this illustrative contrast.

In 1665 Walton wrote his Life of Hooker, less a labor of love than the others, but containing that homely picture of him reading Horace as he tended his scanty sheep, and called away by his wife to rock the cradle. In 1670 came the Life of Herbert, written, he tells us, chiefly to please himself. Some time before 1678, it is uncertain when, his daughter Anne became the wife of the Reverend William Hawkins, one of the prebends of Winchester, and with them he seems to have spent his latter years. In that year he wrote the Life of Sanderson, which, as showing no sign of mental disrepair, is surely an almost unparalleled feat for a man of eighty-five. Length of days is one of the blessings of the Old Testament, and surely it might be added to the Beatitudes of the New, when, as with Walton, it means only a longer ripening, a more abundant leisure to look backwards without self-reproach, and forwards with an assured gratitude to God for a future goodness like the past. There is, perhaps, if we condescend to a purely utilitarian view, no stronger argument for belief in a personal Deity than that it makes possible this ennobling sense of gratitude;

and in a time when such possibility has been so largely analyzed and refined away, Walton's habitual recognition of so direct and conscious an obligation that he cannot resist the interjectional expression of it is a chief cause of the solace and refreshment we feel in reading him. As we read we inhale an odor from the leaves as if flowers from the garden of childhood had been pressed between them, and for a moment, by the sweet sophistry of association, we stand again among them where they grew. Here is incontaminate piety, wholesome as bread. It is a gush of involuntary emotion like that first sincere and precious juice which their own weight forces from the grapes. A fine morning, a meadow flushed with primroses, are not only good in themselves, but sweeter and better because they give him occasion to be thankful for them. We may be wiser, but it may be doubted whether we are so happy, in our self-reliant orphanhood. He had two pleasures where we have but one, and that one doubtingly now that the shadow of the metaphysic cloud has darkened Nature.

In 1683 Walton published "Thealma and Clearchus, a pastoral history in smooth and easie verse written long since by John Chalkhill, Esq., an acquaintant and friend of Edmund Spencer" [*sic*]. The preface is dated five years earlier. The poem is incomplete, with this quaint note by Walton at the end: "And here the author died, and I hope the reader will be sorry." When Mr. S. W. Singer reprinted it in 1820 he expressed his doubts whether such a person as John Chalkhill had ever existed, and his strong suspicion that it might be a youthful production of Walton himself. But several John (or Jon) Chalkhills have since been unearthed; one of them (who died in 1615) being remotely connected with Walton through the marriage of his daughter with one of the Kens. Sir Harris Nicolas, who rejects Mr. Singer's suspicion as implying a duplicity of which honest Izaak would have been incapable, drolly enough fixes upon another John Chalkhill, Fellow of Winchester College, as the probable author of the poem. This he does with Walton's statement that the author was "an acquaintant and friend" of Spenser, and that of John Chalkhill's monument in Winchester Cathedral that he died in 1679, *octogenarius*, both before him. Now Spenser died in 1599; and *this* Chalkhill, at least, could not have known him. But if the other, who died in 1615, wrote "Thealma and Clearchus," he certainly did not write it as it was printed by Walton. The language is altogether too modern for that, unless, indeed, he was endowed with a spirit of prophecy that both foresaw and forestalled the changes in his mother-tongue. The invariable use of the possessive *its* and the elision of the *e* in the past participle would be conclusive. The tone is also too modern, though this is more easily to be felt than defined in words. While there is nothing that compels us to accept Mr. Singer's suggestion as to the authorship, it is certain that the poem has been largely rewritten by somebody, and this must have been Walton. It

has many of the characteristics of his style, — his
discursiveness, his habit of leaving the direct track
of narrative on the suggestion of the first inviting
by-path. his commonplaceness of invention, and,
what is even more suspicious, the same imperfect
rhymes, sometimes mere assonances, which are
found in verses admittedly his own. I find also,
or think I find, unmistakable (though veiled) allu-
sions to the Civil War consonant with some that
Walton could not refrain in his acknowledged
writings. There is almost nothing in it that suggests poetry. Indeed, I remember but a single
happy phrase: —

> " in the proud deep
> She and her bold Clearchus sweetly sleep
> In those soft beds of darkness."

There is another passage worth quoting as applicable to Walton himself in his old age: —

> " And he was almost grown a child again.
> Yet sound in judgment, not impaired in mind,
> For age had rather the soul's parts refined
> Than any way infirmed. his wit no less
> Than 't was in youth. his memory as fresh;
> He failed in nothing but his earthly part
> That tended to its centre, yet his heart
> Was still the same and beat as lustily."

And in his preface Walton perfectly describes himself in describing the real or imaginary author: —

> ·· He was in his time a man generally known and as
> well beloved ; for he was humble and obliging in his be-
> havior, a gentleman. a scholar, very innocent and pru-
> dent; and indeed his whole life was useful, quiet, and
> virtuous."

I am convinced that "Thealma and Clearchus," whoever may have sketched it, is mainly Walton's as it now stands, and I believe it to be the work of his middle or later life. The gap of five years between the date of the preface and that of publication is hard to explain if we suppose him to have been merely the editor. The hesitation of an author venturing himself, even under an alias, in a new direction, seems a more natural explanation. If he was the author, I cannot agree with Archdeacon Nares and Sir Harris Nicolas that the artifice was very culpable, or that Walton would have thought it so. The evidence internal and external that he was author of the two letters from "a quiet and comfortable [conformable?] citizen in London to two busy and factious shopkeepers in Coventry," published in 1680, and signed R. W., seems to me conclusive. Had he attributed to Chalkhill a poem as bad in its morals as "Thealma and Clearchus" in its verse, it would have been quite another matter. Walton thought the poem good, or he would not have published it; and the worst harm that could come to Chalkhill would be the reputation of being a bad poet, — not very hard to bear with so many to keep him in countenance, and he safe under the sod for sixty-eight years.

Whether author or editor, Walton did not live long to enjoy the mystification or share the success, if any there were. He wrote his own will in October, 1683; and on the 15th December of that year, to borrow the words of his granddaughter's epitaph, written no doubt by himself, he died in the ninetieth year "of his innocency."

In his will there is this remarkable passage:
" My worldly estate, which I have nether got by
falsehood or flattery, or the extreme crewelty of the
law of this nation." This cruelty, I have no doubt,
was the power which the law put into the hands
of evil landlords. On this subject Walton held
opinions which, if put in practice, would have
prevented the social miseries of Ireland and the
consequent political retribution which England is
compelled to suffer for them. This is all the more
creditable to him because he was by temperament
and principle conservative, and not only a friend to
that order of the Universe which was by law established in Church and State, but a lover of it. He
tells of a pitiless landlord who was a parishioner of
Sanderson, and of Sanderson's successful dealing
with him, and adds: —

" It may be noted that in this age there are a sort of
people so unlike the God of Mercy, so void of the bow-
els of pity, that they love only themselves and children,
love them so as not to be concerned whether the rest of
mankind waste their days in sorrow and shame, — people that are cursed with riches and a mistake that nothing but riches can make them and theirs happy."

The character of Walton's friendships and his
fidelity to them when prorogued by death bear ample witness to the fine quality of his nature. How
amiably human it was he betrays at every turn,
yet with all his *bonhomie* there is a dignity which
never forgets itself or permits us to forget it. We
may apply to him what he says of Sir Henry
Wotton's father: that he was "a man of great

modesty, of a most plain and single heart, of an
ancient freedom and integrity of mind," and may
say of him, as he says of Sir Henry himself, that
he had "a most persuasive behavior." His friends
loved to call him "honest Izaak." He speaks of
his own "simplicity and harmlessness," and tells
us that his humor was "to be free and pleasant and
civilly merry," and that he "hated harsh censures."
He makes it a prime quality of the gentleman to be
"communicable." He had no love of money, and
compassionates those who are "condemned to be
rich." He was a staunch royalist and church-
man, loved music, painting, good ale, and a pipe,
and takes care to tell us that a certain artificial
fly " was made by a handsome woman and with a
fine hand." But what justifies and ennobles these
lower loves, what gives him a special and native
aroma like that of Alexander, is that above all he
loved the beauty of holiness and those ways of taking and of spending life that make it wholesome
for ourselves and our fellows. His view of the
world is not of the widest, but it is the Delectable
Mountains that bound the prospect. Never surely
was there a more lovable man, nor one to whom
love found access by more avenues of sympathy.

There are two books which have a place by
themselves and side by side in our literature, —
Walton's "Complete Angler" and White's "Natural History of Selborne;" and they are books,
too, which have secured immortality without showing any tincture of imagination or of constructive
faculty, in the gift of one or the other of which that

distinction commonly lies. They neither stimulate
thought nor stir any passionate emotion. If they
make us wiser, it is indirectly and without attempting it, by making us more cheerful. The purely
literary charm of neither of them will alone au-
thorize the place they hold so securely, though, as
respects the "Angler," this charm must be taken
more largely into account. They cannot be called
popular, because they attract only a limited number of readers, but that number is kept full by new
recruits in every generation; and they have survived
every peril to which editing could expose them,
even the crowning one of illustration. They have
this in common, that those who love them find
themselves growing more and more to love the authors of them too. Theirs is an immortality of
affection, perhaps the most desirable, as it is the
rarest, of all. I do not mean that there are no
books in other languages, and no other books in our
own, that invite to a similar intimacy and inspire
the same enthusiasm of regard. "Don Quixote"
and "Elia" appeal to the memory at once. But
in both of these there is also the sorcery of genius,
there is the touch of the master, as well as the shy
personal attractiveness of the writer. In the two
books of which I have been speaking, what prima-
rily interests us is the unconscious revelation of the
authors' character; and it is through the kindly
charm of this and a certain homely inspiration
drawn from the sources of every-day experience
that they tighten their hold upon us. Nature had
endowed these men with the simple skill to make

happiness out of the cheap material that is within the means of the poorest of us. The good fairy gave them to weave cloth of gold out of straw. They did not waste their time or strive to show their cleverness in discussing whether life were worth living, but found every precious moment of it so without seeking, or made it so without grimace, and with no thought that they were doing anything worth remark. Both these books are pre-eminently cheerful books, and have the invaluable secret of distilling sunshine out of leaden skies. They are companionable books, that tempt us out-of-doors and keep us there. The reader of the "Angler" especially finds himself growing conscious of one meaning in the sixth Beatitude too often overlooked, — that the pure in heart shall see God, not only in some future and far-off sense, but wherever they turn their eyes.

I have hesitated to say that Walton had style, because, though that quality, the handmaid of talent and the helpmeet of genius, have left the unobtrusive traces of its deft hand in certain choicer parts of Walton's writing, — his guest-chambers as it were, — yet it does by no means pervade and regulate the whole. For in a book we feel the influence of style everywhere, though we never catch it at its work, as in a house we divine the neat-handed ministry of woman. Walton too often leaves his sentences in a clutter. But there are other qualities which, if they do not satisfy like style, are yet even more agreeable, draw us nearer to an author, and make us happier in him. Why try to discover

what the charm of a book is, if only it charm?   If
I must seek a word that more than any other explains the pleasure which Walton's way of writing
gives us, I should say it was its innocency.   It re-
freshes like the society of children.   I do not know
whether he had humor, but there are passages that
suggest it, as where, after quoting Montaigne's delightful description of how he played with his cat,
he goes on: "Thus freely speaks Montaigne concerning cats," as if he had taken an undue liberty
with them; or where he makes a meteorologist of
the crab, that "at a certain age gets into a dead
fish's shell, and like a hermit dwells there alone
studying the wind and weather;" or where he tells
us of the palmer-worm, that "he will boldly and
disorderly wander up and down, and not endure
to be kept to a diet or fixed to a particular place."
And what he says of Sanderson — that "he did
put on some faint purposes to marry" — would
have arrided Lamb.   These, if he meant to be
droll, have that seeming inadvertence which gives
its highest zest to humor and makes the eye twinkle
with furtive connivance.   Walton's weaknesses,
too, must be reckoned among his other attractions.
He praises a meditative life, and with evident sin-
cerity; but we feel that he liked nothing so well as
good talk.   His credulity leaves front and back
door invitingly open.   For this I rather praise than
censure him, since it brought him the chance of a
miracle at any odd moment, and this complacency
of belief was but a lower form of the same quality
of mind that in more serious questions gave him his

equanimity of faith. And how persuasively beautiful that equanimity is! Heaven was always as real to him as to us are countries we have seen only in the map, and so near that he caught wafts of the singing there when the wind was in the right quarter. I must not forget Walton's singular and genuine love of Nature and his poetical sympathy with it, less common then than now when "all have got the seed." This love was not in the Ercles vein such as is now in fashion, but tender and true, and expresses itself not deliberately but in caressing ejaculations, as where he speaks of "the little living creatures with which the sun and summer adorn and beautify the river-banks and meadows . . . whose life, they say, Nature intended not to exceed an hour, and yet that life is made shorter by other flies or by accident." What far-reaching pity in this concluding sigh, and how keen a sense of the sweetness of life, too! In one respect, I think, he is peculiar, — his sensitiveness to odors. In enumerating the recreations of man, he reckons sweet smells among them. It is Venator who says this, to be sure; but in the "Angler" there is absolutely no dramatic sense, and it is always Walton who speaks. A part of our entertainment, indeed, is to see him doubling so many parts and all the while so unmistakably himself.

Walton certainly cannot be called original in the sense that he opened new paths to thought or new vistas to imagination. Such men are rare, but almost as rare are those who have force enough of nature to suffuse whatever they write with their own individuality and to make a thought fresh again and their own by the addition of this indefinable supplement. This constitutes literary originality, and this Walton had. Whatever entered his mind or memory came forth again *plus* Izaak Walton. We have borrowed of the Latin mythology the word " genius " to express certain intellectual powers or aptitudes which we are puzzled to define, so elusive are they. I have already admitted that this term in its ordinary acceptation cannot be applied to Walton. This would imply larger "draughts of intellectual day " than his ever were or could be. For we ordinarily confine it to a single species of power, which seems sometimes (as in Villon, Marlowe, and Poe) wholly dissociated from the rest of the man, and continues to haunt the ruins of him with its superior presence as if it were rather a *genius loci* than the *natale comes qui temperat astrum*. In Walton's case, since a Daimon or a Genius would be too lofty for the business, might we not take the Brownie of our own Northern mythology for the type of such superior endowment as he clearly had? We can fancy him ministered to by such a homely and helpful creature, — not a genius exactly, but answering the purpose sufficiently well, and marking a certain natural distinction in those it singles out for its innocent and sportful companionship. And it brings a blessing also to those who treat it kindly, as Walton did.

Fortunate senex, ergo tua rura manebunt.

DURING the hurly-burly of the English Civil War, which made the bee in every man's bonnet buzz all the more persistently to be let forth, whoever would now write to his newspaper was driven, for want of that safety-valve, to indite a pamphlet, and, as he believed that the fate of what for the moment was deemed the Universe hung on his opinion, was eager to make it public ere the opportune moment should be gone by forever. Every one of these enthusiasts felt as Robert Owen did when he said to Wilberforce, "What, Sir, would you put off the happiness of Mankind till the next session of Parliament?" Every crotchet and whimsey, too, became the nucleus of a sect, and, as if Old England could not furnish enough otherwise-mindedness of her own, New England sent over Rogers and Gorton to help in the confusion of tongues. All these sects, since each singly was in a helpless and often hateful minority, were united in the assertion of their right to freedom of opinion and to the uncurtailed utterance of whatever they fancied that opinion to be. Many of them, it should seem, could hardly fail in their mental vagabondage to stumble upon the principle of universal toleration, but none discovered anything more novel than that Liberty of Prophesying is good for Me and very bad for Thee. It is remarkable how beautiful the countenance of Toleration always looks in this partial view of it, but it is conceivable that any one of these heterodoxies, once in power and therefore orthodox, would have buckled round all dissenters the strait-waistcoat yet warm from the constraint of more precious limbs. Indeed, this inconsistency, so concise a proof of the consistency of human nature, was illustrated when the General Court of Massachusetts suppressed the first attempt at a newspaper in 1690, and forbade the printing of anything "without licence first obtained from those appointed by the Government to grant the same." Williams, as was natural in one of his amiable temper, was more generous than the rest, but even he lived long enough to learn that there were politico-theological bores in Rhode Island so sedulous and so irritating that they made him doubt the efficacy of his own nostrum, just as the activity of certain domestic insects might make a Brahmin waver as to the sacredness of life in some of its lower organisms.

The prevailing Party had also its jangling minorities whose criticisms and arguments and complaints it was convenient to suppress, and accordingly Parliament, in June, 1643, passed an Ordinance to restrain unlicensed printing. They had so little learned how to use their newly acquired freedom as to be certain that they could compel other men to the right use of theirs. This is not to be wondered at, for even democracies are a great while in finding out that everything may be left to the instincts of a free people save those instincts themselves, and that these, docile if guided gently, grow mutinous under unskilful driving.   Parliament was trying no new experiment, for the press, as if it were an animal likely to run mad and bite somebody at any moment, had been muzzled since Queen Mary's day, but they were trying over again, as men are wont, an experiment that had always failed, and in the nature of things always must fail.

Unwise repression made evasion only the more actively ingenious, and gave it that color of righteousness which is the most dangerous consequence of ill-considered legislation.   Counsel was darkened by a swarm of pamphlets surreptitiously brooded in cellars and cocklofts.   Fancy sees their authors fluttering round the New Light on dingy quarto wings and learning that Truth incautiously approached can singe as well as shine.   Every doctrine inconceivable by instructed men was preached, and the ghost of every dead and buried heresy did squeak and gibber in the London streets.   The right of private misjudgment had been exercised so fantastically on the Scriptures that thoughtful persons were beginning to surmise whether there were not enough explosive material between their covers to shatter any system of government or of society that ever was or will be contrived by man. All this was the natural result of circumstances wholly novel, of a universal ferment of thought or

of its many plausible substitutes, enthusiasm, fanaticism, monomania, and every form of mental
and moral bewilderment suddenly loosed from the
unconscious restraints of traditional order. Those
who watched the strange intellectual and ethico-
political upheaval in New England fifty years ago
will be at no loss for parallels to these phenomena.
It was a state of things that should have been left
to subside, as it had arisen, through natural causes;
but the powers that be always think themselves
wiser than the laws of Nature or the axioms of
experience.

Two formalities were necessary for the lawful
publication of any printed sheet. These were the
long-established entry at Stationers' Hall and the
license required by the new Ordinance. Men in a
hurry to save the world before night, dissident as
they might be in other respects, were agreed in re-
senting these impediments and delays, and this the
more, doubtless, because of the fees they exacted.
Milton, who had nothing in common with such men
except the belief in a divine mission, had in publishing his controversial tracts quietly ignored both
the rights of the Stationers and the injunctions of
the Ordinance. As respects the Stationers' Company, he should have complied with the law, since
entry in their register was the only security for
copyright, and he believed, as he tells us in his
"Iconoclastes," that "every author should have
the property in his work reserved to him after
death as well as living." It was the infringement
of their copyrights by piratical printers during the

general confusion, which seems first to have moved the Stationers' Company to protest against the general violation of the laws controlling the press. Milton's tract on Divorce, published, like others of his before, without license or registry, had made a scandal even among those who regarded a breach of the Seventh Commandment as the only effective liniment for the sprains and bruises of matrimony. And indeed Milton had ventured very far in that dangerous direction where liberty is apt to shade imperceptibly into the warmer hues of license, though not so cynically far as Lady Mary Wortley Montagu afterwards went in her proposed septennial rearrangement. The Stationers seized the opportunity to denounce him twice by name, first to a committee of the Commons, and then to a committee of the Lords. Nothing seems to have come of their complaints, and indeed the attention of both houses must have been too much absorbed by more serious warfare to find time for engaging in this Battle of the Books. Nothing came of them, that is to say, on the part of Parliament, but on Milton's came the "Areopagitica."

We are indebted to the painstaking and fruitful researches of Mr. Masson for a more precise knowledge of the particulars which bring this tract into closer and clearer relations with the personal interests of Milton, and some such nearer concern was always needed as a motive to give his prose, in which, as he says, he worked only with his left hand, its fullest energy and vivacity. Nor is this the case with his prose only. It is true also of his

verse in those passages which are the most characteristically his own. Perhaps he himself was dimly
conscious of this, for in his "Doctrine and Discipline of Divorce " he says that "when points of difficulty are to be discussed, appertaining to the removal of unreasonable wrong and burthen from the
perplexed life of our brothers, it is incredible how
cold, how dull, and how far from all fellow-feeling
we are without the spur of self-concernment." In
the "Areopagitica," he was not only advocating
certain general principles, but pleading his own
cause. The largeness of the theme absolves the
egotism of the motive, while this again adds fervor
to the argument and penetration to the voice of the
advocate. The "Areopagitica" is the best known
and most generally liked of Milton's prose writings,
because it is the only one concerning whose subject
the world has more nearly come to an agreement.
In all the others except the tract concerning Education, and the "History of Britain" in its first edition, there are embers of controversy which the
ashes of two centuries cover but have not cooled.

There is a passage in his "Second Defence "
where Milton speaks of the "Areopagitica " as one
section of a tripartite scheme which he had thought
out "to the promotion of real and substantial liberty." After giving a list of his writings on matters ecclesiastic, he says, "When, therefore, I
perceived that there were three species of liberty
without which scarcely any life can be completely
led, religious, domestic or private, and civil, as I
had already written concerning the first, and the

magistrates were strenuously active concerning the third, I took to myself the second or domestic. And, as this seemed tripartite, if marriage, if the education of children were to be as they should, if there should be liberty of philosophizing, I set forth my opinion not only concerning the rightful con- tracting of marriage, but also the dissolving thereof, if it should be necessary. . . . I then treated more briefly of the education of children in a single small work. . . . And lastly concerning the freeing of the press, lest the judgment of true and false, of what should be published, what suppressed, should be in the power of a few men of little learn- ing and of vulgar judgment, . . . I wrote in the proper style of an oration the 'Areopagitica.' "

The sub-title of this work accordingly is "a speech for the liberty of unlicenced printing," but it is much more than this.   It is a plea in behalf of freedom of research in all directions (*libertas phi- losophandi*), and there is in it implicitly the doc- trine of universal toleration.   But Milton's inten- tion had no such scope as that, for it is plain from what he says elsewhere that he would have drawn the line on this side of Popery, of atheism, and most probably of whatever was immediately incon- venient to so firm a believer as he was in the infal- libility of John Milton.   Such was the irony of Fate that he himself a few years later became a censor of the press.   It was perhaps with an eye to this comic property of the whirligig of Time that he wrote the passage just quoted from the "Second Defence," in which it is implied that some things should be suppressed. But Milton was not inconsistent with himself, however he might be so with the principles advocated in the "Areopagitica," as those who have studied his character know. He is never weary of insisting on the Tacitean distinction between liberty and license, and in his "History of Britain" says admirably well "that liberty hath a sharp and double edge fit only to be handled by just and virtuous men: to bad and dissolute it becomes a mischief unwieldy in their own hands." And if consistency be a jewel, as the proverb affirms, yet it can only show its best lustre in a suitable setting of circumstances. Milton was always a champion of freedom as he understood it, a freedom "not to be won from without, but from within, in the right conduct and administration of life." Toland speaks of him as favoring "the erection of a perfect Democracy," but in truth no man was ever farther from being a democrat in the modern sense than he. The government that he preferred would have been that of a Council chosen by a strictly limited body of constituents and this indirectly, their function being only to choose electors who again should make choice of a smaller body, and so on through "a third or fourth sifting and refining of exactest choice." His scheme aimed at the establishment of something like a Venetian Republic without a Doge, his experience of Cromwell apparently having made any monocratic devices distasteful to him. For the "rude multitude," as he calls it, he had an unqualified contempt, and had no more belief in the divine right

of majorities than in that of tyrants. Undoubt-
edly when a man of Milton's temperament advocated free speech it was with the unconscious mental reservation that it should be on the right side,
or, at any rate, that it should be speech and not
jargon.

There is no trustworthy evidence that the "Areopagitica" produced any immediate effect, unless it
may have been indirectly by leavening some small
fraction of the sluggish lump of what we should
now call public opinion. Interests more immediate
and pressing must soon have crowded it out of
mind, and in a few years the returning flood of
royalism covered it, with the other prose works of
Milton, in a deepening ooze of oblivion. So
utterly must it have been forgotten that in 1693
Charles Blount boldly plagiarized it under the new
title of " A Just Vindication of Learning and the
Liberty of the Press by Philopatris," in which he
had the impudence to quote a passage from the
very book he was rifling with the condescending
remark "Herein I agree with Mr. Milton," as if
it were an exception to his general way of thinking.
Whether the tract in this vulgarized form helped
forward the cause in behalf of which it was written
is matter of conjecture. None of Blount's pamphlets could have had any considerable vent, for
when Gildon published "The Miscellaneous Works
of Charles Blount, Esq.," it is evident that he
merely bound together the several pieces which
made up the volume, putting new title-pages to all
save one of them, but leaving the old pagination of

each. There must therefore have been enough un-
sold copies to serve the needs of this edition. Be
this as it may, Blount, by means of a scurvy trick
played on the licenser, Bohun,— a trick one is half
inclined to forgive because of its genuine humor and
its beneficent results, — was the immediate cause
of events which led to the final abandonment of the
licensing system. A full account of the affair may
be found in Macaulay's History, where the facts
were for the first time unearthed. Macaulay, as
is his wont in dealing with men whom he dislikes,
blackens the character of Blount more than it deserves, and underrates his ability. He was not an
atheist, though, for the point of the historian's an-
tithesis, he ought to have been, and he certainly had
more than the talents of a third-rate pamphleteer.
He did not live to see the triumph of his cause.
It would be pleasant to associate Milton even indirectly with that triumph, as we might if we could
suppose that the "Areopagitica" had first awakened
Blount's interest in the freedom of the press. But
in point of fact his quarrel with the licensers was
an old one, and he merely picked up Milton's tract
as he would a handy stone to throw at the dog he
was pelting. After an interval of forty years the
"Areopagitica" was reprinted with a preface by
Thomson the poet, when it was proposed once more
to put a bridle on the press.

It cannot be said that the prose works of Milton
have ever been in any sense popular, or read by
any public much more numerous than the proof-
reader. So far as they are concerned, Milton has

had his wish and his audience has only been too few, whether fit or not. They do not appear to have tempted even the omnivorous Coleridge in his maturer years, though traces of their influence may be surmised in his earlier prose. It is curious that no notes upon them are to be found in his "Literary Remains," and but a single brief remark in his "Table-talk," to the effect that Milton's style was better in Latin than in English. I find no evident signs of contagion from them in any great writers of English except Burke, who has caught both their qualities and their defects, unless, indeed, the likeness spring from their both having modelled themselves on Cicero. Since 1698, when Toland published the first edition of them in Holland, they have been only four times reprinted. Nor is this want of interest to be explained by the fact that their matter is mainly contentious and polemical, for they discuss questions whose roots strike deeply into the bedrock of politics and morals, and where they find a crevice widen it into an irreconcilable cleavage of opinion. The reason must be sought, then, not so much in their substance as in their method and manner. They are indeed for the most part the impassioned harangues of a supremely eloquent man, full of matter, but careless of the form in which he utters it; rich in learning, but too intent on the constant display of it with the cumbrous prodigality of one to whom such wealth is new. He had no doubt a manner of his own, and boasts that by means of it the authorship of his treatise on Divorce was detected when printed anonymously. And in his "Reason of Church-government urged against Prelaty" he says, "Whether aught was imposed me by them that had the overlooking, or betaken to of mine own choice in English or other tongue, prosing or versing, but chiefly by this latter, the style, by certain vital signs it had, was likely to live." Time has proved this to be true of his verse, but not so of his prose. For in truth his prose has no style in the higher sense, as, for instance, the "Religio Medici" has. There are passages, to be sure, which for richness of texture, harmony of tone, and artistic distribution of parts, can hardly be matched in our language, but that equable distinction which is the constant note of his verse is wanting. A sentence builded majestically with every help of art and imagination too often thrusts heavenward from a huddle of vulgar pentices such as used to cluster about mediæval cathedrals. Never was such inequality. It is as if some transcendent voice in mid soar of the Kyrie Eleison should drop into a comic song. His sentences are often loutish and difficult, in controversy he is brutal, and at any the most inopportune moment capable of an incredible coarseness. Let a single instance from his "Reformation in England" suffice, where he speaks of "that queasy temper of lukewarmness that gives a vomit to God himself." Jeremy Taylor is often coarse, but never to the degree of disgust. Strangely enough, too, Milton is careless of euphony, seeming to prefer words not only low but harsh, and such cacophonous superla-

tives as "virtuousest," "viciousest," "sheepishest,"
even making the last two hiss in the same sentence.
Perhaps he is at his worst when he fancies that he
is being playful and humorous (dangerous tight-
ropes for an insupportable foot like his), and, as
he says in his "Animadversions upon the Remon-
strant's Defence," "mixes here and there a grim
laughter such as may appear at the same time in
an austere visage." Grim laughter it is indeed.
Too often also he blusters, and we are forced to
condone in him, as he in Luther, "how far he gave
way to his own fervent mind." It does not satisfy
us to excuse these faults as common to the time,
for Milton himself has taught us to expect of him
that choice of language and that faultless marshal-
ling of it which is of all time, and sometimes even
in his prose there are periods which have all the
splendor, all the dignity, and all the grave exhilaration of his verse. Some virtue of his singing-
robes seems left, as if they had not long been
doffed.

As a master of harmony and of easily-maintained
elevation in English blank verse Milton has no
rival. He was skilled in many tongues and many
literatures; he had weighed the value of words,
whether for sound or sense, or where the two may
be of mutual help. He surely, if any, was what
he calls "a mint-master of language." He must
have known, if any ever knew, that even in the
"sermo pedestris" there are yet great differences
in gait, that prose is governed by laws of modula-
tion as exact if not so exacting as those of verse,

and that it may conjure with words as prevailingly. The music is secreted in it, yet often more potent in suggestion than that of any verse which is not of utmost mastery. We hearken after it as to a choir in the side chapel of some cathedral heard faintly and fitfully across the long desert of the nave, now pursuing and overtaking the cadences, only to have them grow doubtful again and elude the ear before it has ceased to throb with them. A prose sentence, then, only fulfils its entire function when, as in some passages of the English version of the Old Testament, its rhythm so keeps time and tune with the thought or feeling that the reader is guided to the accentuation of the writer as securely as if in listening to his very voice. The fifth chapter of the Book of Judges is crowded with these triumphs of well-measured words. Are we not made to see as with our eyes the slow collapse of Sisera's body, as life and will forsake it, and then to hear his sudden fall at last in the dull thud of "he fell down dead," where every word sinks lower and lower, to stop short with the last? There are many noble periods in Milton's prose, and they are noble in a way where he is without competitors, for surely he is the most eloquent of Englishmen. But there are a half-dozen men either his contemporaries, or nearly so, whose prose is far more evenly good than his and above all moves with a practised ease in which his is wholly wanting. He prevails even with the ear less often than Browne, and almost never stirs the imagination through the ear as Browne has the art to do.

He is too eagerly intent on his argument to linger over the artifices by which it might be more
winningly set forth.   He has been taxed with Lat-
inism, and oddly enough by Doctor Johnson, who
I feel sure could not have read any one of his
tracts, unless it were the "Areopagitica," for very
wrath.   He has, it is true, some Latin construc-
tions and uses a few words (like "assert," "pre-
varicator," "disoblige ") in their radical rather
than in their derivative meaning, but on the whole
his language is less vitiated with verbs taken directly from the Latin than that of most of the
writers coeval with him.   The much overrated
Feltham, for instance, "formicates " with them, as
he would have called·it, and one might almost learn
Latin by reading the "Vulgar Errors."   It is
Milton's English words rather that seem foreign
to us, such as "disgospel," "disworship," "disal-
leige," "lossless," "natureless," or "underfoot "
and "lifeblood" used as adjectives.   Sometimes
he ventures on what would now be called an Ameri-
canism, as where he tells us of a "loud stench."
But the most obvious defect of his prose is, as I
have hinted, its want of equanimity.

He is not so truly a writer of great prose as a
great man writing in prose, and it is really Milton
that we seek there more than anything else.   He
is great enough when we find him to repay a thou-
sand-fold what the search may have cost us.   And
when we meet him at his best, there is something
in his commerce that fortifies the mind as only
contact with a great character can.   He is then a

perpetual fountain of highmindedness. In contest with an adversary he is brutally willing to strike below the belt, and shows as little magnanimity or fairness as the average editor of an American newspaper in dealing with a political opponent. Even Voltaire, hardened as were his own controversial nerves, was shocked by the nature of the weapons which Milton was eager to employ against Morus. But when he recovers possession of his true self, he is so at home among those things that endure, so amply conversant with whatever is of good report, so intimately conscious of a divine presence in a world of doubt and failure and disillusion, and of those spiritual ministrations symbolized by the prophet in the wilderness, that we listen to him as Adam to the angel, and the voice lingers not only in the ear but in the life. Mr. James Grant in his "Newspaper Press" says, drolly enough, of Coleridge, that "there was to the latest hour of his life a tendency, which could not be sufficiently deplored, to soar into regions of unrevealed truth." It is this lift in Milton, rare enough among men, this undying instinct to soar and tempt us to venture our weaker wing, that gives an incomparable efficacy to those parts of his writing in prose that are best inspired. Here we breathe a mountain air in which, as Rousseau says, " à mesure qu'on approche des régions éthérées l'âme contracte quelque chose de leur inaltérable pureté." Nay, even while we are trudging wearily over the low and marish stretches of his discourse. there rises suddenly from before our feet a winged phrase that mounts and carols like a lark, luring the mind with it to ampler spaces and a serener atmosphere. It is no small education for the nobler part of us to consort with one of such temper that he could say of himself with truth, "God intended to prove me, whether I durst take up alone a rightful cause against a world of disesteem, and found I durst." And it is the breath of this spirit that pours through the "Areopagitica" as through a trumpet, sounding the charge against whatever is base and recreant, whether in the world about us or in the ambush of our own natures.

SHAKESPEARE'S "RICHARD III."

AN ADDRESS READ BEFORE THE EDINBURGH PHILOSOPHI-
CAL INSTITUTION.

1883.

AFTER a general introduction, Mr. Lowell
said : —

I propose to say a few words on one of the plays
usually attributed to Shakespeare, — a play in respect of which I find myself in the position of Peter
Bell, seeing little more than an ordinary primrose
where I ought, perhaps, to see the plant and flower
of light; I mean the play of "Richard III." Horace Walpole wrote "Historic Doubts" concerning
the monarch himself, and I shall take leave to
express some about the authorship of the drama
that bears his name. I have no intention of applying to it a system of subjective criticism which I
consider as untrustworthy as it is fascinating, and
which I think has often been carried beyond its legitimate limits. But I believe it absolutely safe to
say of Shakespeare that he never wrote deliberate
nonsense, nor was knowingly guilty of defective me-
tre; yet even tests like these I would apply with
commendable modesty and hesitating reserve, conscious that the meaning of words, and still more

the associations they call up, have changed since Shakespeare's day; that the accentuation of some was variable, and that Shakespeare's ear may very likely have been as delicate as his other senses. On the latter point, however, I may say in passing, of his versification, which is often used as a test for the period of his plays, that Coleridge, whose sense of harmony and melody was perhaps finer than that of any other modern poet, did not allow his own dramatic verse the same licenses, and I might almost say the same mystifications, which he esteems applicable in regulating or interpreting that of Shakespeare. This is certainly remarkable. For my own part, I am convinced that if we had Shakespeare's plays as he wrote them, — and not as they have come down to us, deformed by the careless hurry of the copiers-out of parts, by the emendations of incompetent actors, and the mishearings of shorthand writers,— I am convinced that we should not find from one end of them to the other a demonstrably faulty verse or a passage obscure for any other reason than depth of thought or supersubtlety of phrase.

I know that in saying this I am laying myself open to the reproach of applying common sense to a subject which of all others demands uncommon sense for its adequate treatment, — demands perception as sensitive and divination as infallible as the operations of that creative force they attempt to measure are illusive and seemingly abnormal. But in attempting to answer a question like that I have suggested, I should be guided by considerations far less narrow. We cannot identify printed thoughts by the same minute comparisons that would serve to convict the handwriting of them. To smell the rose is surely quite otherwise convincing than to number its petals; and in estimating that sum of qualities which we call character, we trust far more to general than to particular impressions. In guessing at the authorship of an anonymous book. like Southey's "Doctor" or Bulwer's "Timon," while I might lay some stress on tricks of manner, I should be much less influenced by the fact that many passages were above or below the ordinary level of any author whom I suspected of writing it than by the fact that there was a single passage different in kind from his habitual tone. A man may surpass himself or fall short of himself, but he cannot change his nature. I would not be understood to mean that common sense is always or universally applicable in criticism. — Dr. Johnson's treatment of "Lycidas" were a convincing instance to the contrary; but I confess I find often more satisfactory guidance in the illuminated and illuminating common sense of a critic like Lessing, making sure of one landmark before he moved forward to the next, than in the metaphysical dark lanterns which some of his successors are in the habit of letting down into their own consciousness by way of enlightening ours. Certainly common sense will never suffice for the understanding or enjoyment of "those brave translunary things that the first poets had; " but it is at least a remarkably good prophylactic against mistaking a handsaw for a hawk.

What, then, is the nature of the general considerations which I think we ought to bear in mind
in debating a question like this, — the authenticity
of one of Shakespeare's plays? First of all, and
last of all, I should put style; not style in its narrow sense of mere verbal expression, for that may
change and does change with the growth and training of the man, but in the sense of that something,
more or less clearly definable, which is always and
everywhere peculiar to the man, and either in kind
or degree distinguishes him from all other men, —
the kind of evidence which, for example, makes us
sure that Swift wrote "The Tale of a Tub" and
Scott the "Antiquary," because nobody else could
have done it. *Incessu patuit dea,* and there is a
kind of gait which marks the mind as well as the
body. But even if we took the word "style" in that
narrower sense which would confine it to diction and
turn of phrase, Shakespeare is equally incomparable. Coleridge, evidently using the word in this
sense, tells us: "There's such divinity doth hedge
our Shakespeare round that we cannot even imitate
his style. I tried to imitate his manner in the
'Remorse,' and when I had done, I found I had
been tracking Beaumont and Fletcher, and Massin-
ger instead. It is really very curious." Greene,
in a well-known passage, seems to have accused
Shakespeare of plagiarism, and there are verses,
sometimes even a succession of verses of Greene
himself, of Peele, and especially of Marlowe,
which are comparable, so far as externals go, with
Shakespeare's own. Nor is this to be wondered at

in men so nearly contemporary. In fact, I think
it is evident that to a certain extent the two masters of versification who trained Shakespeare were
Spenser and Marlowe. Some of Marlowe's verses
have the same trick of clinging in the ear as
Shakespeare's. There is, for instance, that famous description of Helen, or rather the exclama-
tion of Faust when he first sees Helen : —

> " Was this the face that launched a thousand ships
> And burned the topless towers of Ilium ? "

one verse of which, if I am not mistaken. lingered
in Shakespeare's ear. But the most characteristic
phrases of Shakespeare imbed themselves in the
very substance of the mind, and quiver, years after,
in the memory like arrows that have just struck and
still feel the impulse of the bow. And no whole
scene of Shakespeare, even in his 'prentice days,
could be mistaken for the work of any other man;
for give him room enough, and he is sure to betray
himself by some quality which either is his alone,
or his in such measure as none shared but he.

I am reminded of a remark of Professor Masson's
which struck me a good deal, — that one day, when
tired with overwork, he took up Dante, and after
reading in it for half an hour or so, he shut the
book and found himself saying to himself, " Well.
this is literature ! " And I think that this may
be applied constantly to the mature Shakespeare,
and, in a great measure, to the young Shakespeare.
Take a whole scene together. and there are sure to
be passages in it of which we can say that they are
really literature in that higher meaning of the word.

It is usual to divide the works of Shakespeare by periods, but it is not easy to do this with even an approach to precision unless we take the higher qualities of structure as a guide. As he matured, his plays became more and more organisms, and less and less mere successions of juxtaposed scenes, strung together on the thread of the plot. In assigning periods too positively, I fancy we are apt to be misled a little by the imperfect analogy of the sister art of painting, and by the first and second manners, as they are called, of its great masters. But manual dexterity is a thing of far slower acquisition than mastery of language or the knack of melodious versification. The fancy of young poets is apt to be superabundant. It is the imagination that ripens with the judgment, and asserts itself as the shaping power in a deeper sense than belongs to it as a mere maker of pictures when the eyes are shut. Young poets, especially if they are great poets, learn the art of verse early, and their poetical vocabulary sins rather by excess than defect. They can pick up and assimilate what is to their purpose with astonishing rapidity. The "Canzoniere" of Dante was, at least in part, written before he was twenty-five; and Keats, dying not older than that, left behind him poems that astonish us as much by their maturity of style and their Attic grace of form as they take the ear captive by their music and the fancy by their opaline beauty of phrase. Shakespeare, surely, was as apt a scholar as Keats. Already in the "Venus and Adonis" we find verses quite as gracious in their interlacing

movement, and as full, almost, of picturesque suggestion, as those of his maturer hand.   For example: —

> " Bid me discourse, I will enchant thine ear,
>   Or like a fairy trip upon the green,
>   Or like a nymph, with long dishevelled hair,
>   Dance on the sands and yet no footing seen."

Shakespeare himself was pleased with these verses,
for a famous speech of Prospero in "The Tempest"
has these lines: —

> " And ye that on the sands with printless feet
>   Do chase the ebbing Neptune, and do fly him
>   When he comes back."

I think it is interesting to find Shakespeare improv-
ing on a phrase of his own: it is something that
nobody else could do.   There is even greater excellence in the Sonnets — "Let me not to the marriage of true minds," and many others.   The thing
in which we should naturally expect Shakespeare
to grow more perfect by practice and observation
would be knowledge of stage effect, and skill in
presenting his subject in the most telling way.

It would be on the side of the dramatist, or of
the playwright, perhaps I had better say, rather
than on the side of the poet, that we should look
for development.   To him, as to Molière, his perfect knowledge of stage-business gave an enormous
advantage.   If he took a play in hand to remodel
it for his company, it would be the experience of
the actor much more than the genius of the poet
that would be called into play.   His work would
lie in the direction probably of curtailment oftener

than of enlargement; and though it is probable that in the immaturer plays attributed to him by Heming and Condell in their edition of 1623 a portion, greater or less, may be his, yet it is hard to believe that he can be called their author in anything like the same sense as we are sure he is the author of those works in which no other hand can be suspected, because no other hand has ever been capable of such mastery.

It must be remembered that we come to the reading of all the plays attributed to Shakespeare with the preconception that they are his. The juggler, if he wishes to give us the impression that a sound comes from a certain direction, long beforehand turns our attention that way, makes us expect it thence, and at last we hear it so. This shows the immense power that a •persuasion of this kind has over the imagination even in regard to a thing so physical as sound, and in things so metaphysical as the plays of Shakespeare it applies with even more force. If we take up a play thinking it is his, it is astonishing how many things we excuse, and how many things we slur over, and so on, for various reasons not very satisfactory, I think, if strictly cross-examined. How easily a preconceived idea that a play is Shakespeare's may mislead even clever and accomplished men into seeing what they expect to see is proved by the number of believers in Ireland's clumsy forgery of Vortigern. It was precisely on the style, in its narrow sense of language and versification, that those too credulous persons based their judgment. The German poet and critic, Tieck, believed in the Shakespearean authorship of all the supposititious plays, and in regard to one of them, at least, "The Yorkshire Tragedy," drew his arguments from the diction. Now, so far as mere words go, the dramatists of Shakespeare's time all drew from the same common fund of vocables. The movement of their verse, so far as it was mechanical, would naturally have many points of resemblance.

As an example of the tests sometimes employed and successfully, but which should not be too implicitly relied upon, I will mention that which is called the double-ending, where there is a superfluous syllable at the end of a line. This is a favorite and often tiresome trick of Fletcher's. But Shakespeare also tried it now and then, as in the choruses of "Henry V.," which are among the finest examples of his merely picturesque writing.

It is possible that the external manner of Shakespeare might have been caught and imitated more or less unconsciously by some of his contemporaries, as it most certainly was in the next generation, notably by Webster and Shirley. Fletcher was almost Shakespeare's equal in poetic sentiment; and Chapman rises sometimes nearly to his level in those exultations of passionate self-consciousness to which the protagonists of his tragedies are lifted in the supreme crisis of their fate. But Fletcher's sentiment seems artificial in comparison, and his fancy never sings at heaven's gate as Shakespeare's so often does, and Chapman's grandeur comes dangerously near to what a friend

would call extravagance and an enemy bombast.[1]
There is a certain dramatic passion in Shakespeare's
versification, too, which we find in no other of his
coevals except Marlowe, and in him far less constantly.   Detached verses, I believe, could be cited
from far inferior men that might well pass as the
handiwork of the great master so far as their merely
poetical quality is concerned; but what I mean by
dramatic passion is that in Shakespeare's best and
most characteristic work the very verse is inter-
penetrated by what is going on in the mind of the
speaker, and its movement hastened or retarded by
his emotion rather than by the ear and choice of the
poet.   Yes, single verses, but of other men, might
be taken for his, but no considerable sequence of
them, and no one of his undoubted plays, taken as
a whole, could ever by any possibility be supposed
to be the creation of any other poet.

It is something very difficult to define, this impression which convinces us without argument and
better than all argument, but it would win the ver-
dict of whatever jury.   If the play of "Cymbeline"
had been lost, for example, and the manuscript
were to be discovered to-morrow, who would doubt
its authorship?   Nay, in this case there are short
passages, single verses and phrases even, that bear
the unmistakable mint-mark of him who alone
could ascend the highest heaven of invention; of

---

[1] In Fletcher's *Faithful Shepherdess*, Amoret tells Perigot that
she loves him

"Dearly as swallows love the early dawn,"

which is certainly charming, but seems much more a felicity of
fancy than to touch the more piercing note of passion.

that magician of whom Dryden said so truly, "Within that circle none dare tread but he." And it is really curious, I may say in passing, — that verse of Dryden reminds me of it, — that almost all the poets who have touched Shakespeare seem to become inspired above themselves. The poem that Ben Jonson wrote in his memory has a splendor of movement about it that is uncommon with him, — a sort of rapture; and Dryden wrote nothing finer than what he wrote about the greatest of poets, nor is any other play of his comparable in quality with "All for Love," composed under Shakespeare's immediate and obvious influence.

There are three special considerations, three eminent and singular qualities of Shakespeare, which more than all, or anything else, I think, set him in a different category from his contemporaries; and it is these that I would apply as tests, not always or commonly, indeed, to single verses or scenes, but to the entire play. It has been said, with truth, of Byron, that there is no great poet who so often falls below himself, and this is no doubt true, within narrower limits, of Shakespeare; but I do not think it would be easy to find a whole scene in any of his acknowledged plays where his mind seems at dead low tide throughout, and lays bare its shallows and its ooze. The first of the three characteristics of which I speak is his incomparable force and delicacy of poetic expression, which can never keep themselves hidden for long, but flash out from time to time like those pulses of pale flame with which the sky throbs at unprophesiable intervals, as if in involuntary betrayal of the coming Northern Lights. Such gleams occur in "Love's Labour's Lost," and still more frequently in "A Midsummer - Night's Dream;" and here I choose my examples designedly from plays which are known to be early, and provably early, though it would be perfectly fair, since it is with natural and not acquired qualities that we are concerned, to pick them from any of his plays. Especially noteworthy, also, I think, are those passages in which a picturesque phrase is made the vehicle, as it were by accident, of some pregnant reflection or profound thought, as, for instance, in "A Midsummer-Night's Dream," where Theseus says: —

> "The lunatic, the lover, and the poet
> Are of imagination all compact."

In all his plays we have evidence that he could not long keep his mind from that kind of overflow. I think it is sometimes even a defect that he is apt to be turned out of his direct course by the first metaphysical quibble, if I may so call it, that pops up in his path; but these, of course, are not the things by which we can judge him.

One of the surest of these detective clews is this continual cropping-up (Goethe would have called it intrusion) of philosophical or metaphysical thought in the midst of picturesque imagery or passionate emotion, as if born of the very ecstasy of the language in which it is uttered. Take, for example, a passage from "The Two Noble Kinsmen" which has persuaded nearly all critics that Shakespeare had a hand in writing that play. It is Arcite's invocation of Mars. Observe how it begins with picture, and then deepens down into a condensed statement of all the main arguments that can be urged in favor of war: —

> "Thou mighty one that with thy power hast turned
> Green Neptune into purple ; whose approach
> Comets forewarn ; whose havoc in vast field
> Unearthèd skulls proclaim ; whose breath blows down
> The teeming Ceres' foison ; who dost pluck
> With hand armipotent from forth blue clouds
> The masoned turrets . . .
> O great corrector of enormous times,
> Shaker of o'er-rank States, thou grand decider
> Of dusty and old titles, that heal'st with blood
> The earth when it is sick, and cur'st the world
> O' th' plurisy of people ! "

The second characteristic, of which I should expect to see some adumbration, at least, in any unmistakable work of Shakespeare would be humor, in which itself, and in the quality of it, he is perhaps more unspeakably superior to his contemporaries than in some other directions, — I mean in the power of pervading a character with humor, creating it out of humor, so to speak, and yet never overstepping the limits of nature or coarsening into caricature. In this no man is or ever was comparable with him but Cervantes. Of this humor we have something more than the premonition in some of his earliest plays.

A third characteristic of Shakespeare is eloquence: and this, of course, we expect to meet with, and do meet with, more abundantly in the historical and semi-historical plays than in those where the intrigue is more private and domestic.

If I were called upon to name any one mark more distinctive than another of Shakespeare's work, it would be this. I do not mean mere oratory, as in Antony's speech over the body of Cæsar, but an eloquence of impassioned thought finding vent in vivid imagery. The speeches seem not to be composed, — they grow; thought budding out of thought, and image out of image, by what seems a natural law of development, but by what is no doubt some subtler process of association in the speaker's mind, always gathering force and impetuosity as it goes, from its own very motion. Take as examples the speeches of Ulysses in "Troilus and Cressida."

I think these are the three qualities — subtlety of poetic expression, humor, and eloquence — which we should expect to find in a play of Shakespeare's, and especially in an historical play. Of each and all of these we find less in "Richard III.," as it appears to me, than in any other of his plays of equal pretensions; for although it is true that in "Richard II." there is no humorous character, the humor of irony is many times present in the speeches of the king after his dethronement. There is a gleam of humor here and there in "Richard III.," as where Richard rebukes Buckingham for saying "'zounds," —

"O do not swear, my Lord of Buckingham;"

and there are many other Shakespearean touches; but the play as a whole appears to me always less than it should be, except in scenic effectiveness, to be reckoned a work from Shakespeare's brain and hand alone, or even mainly, — less in all the qualities and dimensions that are most exclusively and characteristically his. This I think to be conclusive, for, as Goethe says very truly, if there be any defect in the most admirable of Shakespeare's plays, it is that they are more than they should be. The same great critic, speaking of his "Henry IV.," says with equal truth "that, were everything else that has come down to us of the same kind lost, [the arts of] poesy and rhetoric could be recreated out of it."

The first impression made upon us by "Richard III." is that it is thoroughly melodramatic in conception and execution. Whoever has seen it upon the stage knows that the actor of Richard is sure to offend against every canon of taste laid down by Hamlet in his advice to the players. He is sure to tear his passion to rags and tatters; he is sure to split the ears of the groundlings; and he is sure to overstep the modesty of nature with every one of his stage strides. Now, it is not impossible that Shakespeare, as a caterer for the public taste, may have been willing that the groundlings as well as other people should help to fill the coffers of his company, and that the right kind of attraction should accordingly be offered them. It is therefore conceivable that he may have retouched or even added to a poor play which had already proved popular; but it is not conceivable that he should have written an entire play in violation of those principles of taste which we may deduce more or less clearly from everything he wrote.

Then, again, Shakespeare's patriotism is characteristic of his plays. It is quite as intense as that of Burns; and in a play dealing with a subject like that of "Richard III." one would expect to see this patriotism show itself in a rather more pronounced manner than usual, because the battle of Bosworth Field, with which the play ends, ended also a long and tragic series of wars, and established on the throne the grandfather of the sovereign who was reigning when the play was put upon the stage. Now there is one allusion, a sort of prophetic allusion, in this play to the succession of Henry VII.'s descendants to the throne; but if you compare it with the admirable way in which Shakespeare — I grant he was then older and his faculties more mature — has dealt with a similar matter in "Macbeth," in the second scene with the witches, which impresses our imagination almost as much as it does that of the usurper himself; if we consider, moreover, that in the play of "Richard III." there is an almost ludicrous procession of ghosts, — for there are eleven of them who pass through, speaking to Richard on the right and to Richmond on the left, — and if we compare this with Shakespeare's treatment of the supernatural in any of his undoubted plays, I think we shall feel that the inferiority is not one of degree, but one of kind.

I cannot conceive how anybody should believe that Shakespeare wrote the two speeches which are made to their armies by Richard and Richmond respectively. That of Richard is by far the better,

and has something of the true Shakespearean ring
in it, something of his English scorn for the up-
start and the foreigner, notably where he calls
Richmond

> " A milksop, one that never in his life
> Felt so much cold as over shoes in snow,"

but that of his antagonist falls ludicrously flat
to shame his worshippers.   Compare it with the
speech of Henry V. under the walls of Harfleur, or
his reply to Westmoreland.   I can conceive almost
anything of Shakespeare except his being dull
through a speech of twenty lines.   I do not think he
is ever that.   He may be hyperbolical; he may be
this, that, or the other; but whatever it is, his fault
is not that he is dull.   If it were not so late, I
would read to you a passage from an earlier play,
— the speech of Gaunt in "Richard II.;" and I
am glad to refer to this, because it shows in part
that eloquence and that intensity of patriotism
which display themselves whenever they can find or
make an opportunity.

If Shakespeare undertook to remodel an already
existing piece, we should expect to find his hand
in the opening scene — for in these his skill is always noticeable in arresting attention and exciting
interest.   Richard's soliloquy at the beginning of
the play may be his in part, though there is a
clumsiness in Richard's way of declaring himself
a scoundrel, and in the reasons he gives for being
one, which is helplessly ridiculous.   He says : —

> " And therefore — since I cannot prove a lover,
> To entertain these fair, well-spoken days —

I am determinèd to prove a villain,
And hate the idle pleasures of these days."

And yet in the very next scene he wooes and wins
Anne, though both she and Elizabeth had told him
very frankly that they knew he was a devil.   It
would be a mistake to compare this betraying of
himself by Richard with the cynical and almost in-
decent frankness of Iago.   Iago was an Italian of
the Renaissance as Shakespeare might have divined
him through that penetrating psychology of his;
and I have been told that even now Italians who
see Salvini's version of Othello sympathize rather
with Iago than with the Moor, whom they consider
to be a dull-witted fellow, deserving the dupery of
which he was the victim.

Nevertheless "Richard III." is a most effective
acting play.   There are, certainly, what seem to
be unmistakable traces of Shakespeare in some of
the worst scenes, though I am not sure that if the
play had been lost, and should be discovered in our
day, this would pass without question.   The soliloquy of Clarence can hardly be attributed to any
other hand, and there are gleams from time to time
that look like manifest records of his kindling
touch.   But the scolding mob of widow queens,
who make their billingsgate more intolerable by
putting it into bad blank verse, and the childish
procession of eleven ghosts seem to me very little
in Shakespeare's style.   For in nothing, as I have
said, is he more singular and preëminent than in
his management of the supernatural.

I find that my time has got the better of me.

I shall merely ask you to read "Richard III." with attention, and with a comparison such as I have hinted at between this and other plays which are most nearly contemporary with it, and I therefore shall not trouble you with further passages.

It seems to me that an examination of "Richard III." plainly indicates that it is a play which Shakespeare adapted to the stage, making additions, sometimes longer and sometimes shorter; and that, towards the end, either growing weary of his work or pressed for time, he left the older author, whoever he was, pretty much to himself. It would be interesting ⸱⸱ follow out minutely a question of this kind, but that would not be possible within the limits of an occasion like this. It will be enough if I have succeeded in interesting you to a certain extent in a kind of discussion that has at least the merit of withdrawing us for a brief hour from the more clamorous interests and questions of the day to topics which, if not so important, have also a perennial value of their own.

While I believe in the maintenance of classical learning in our universities, I never open my Shakespeare but I find myself wishing that there might be professorships established for the expounding of his works as there used to be for those of Dante in Italy. There is nothing in all literature so stimulating and suggestive as the thought he seems to drop by chance, as if his hands were too full; nothing so cheery as his humor; nothing that laps us in Elysium so quickly as the lovely images which he marries to the music of his verse. He is also a

great master of rhetoric in teaching us what to follow, and sometimes quite as usefully what to avoid.
I value him above all for this: that for those who
know no language but their own there is as much
intellectual training to be got from the study of his
works as from that of the works of any, I had almost said all, of the great writers of antiquity.

THE STUDY OF MODERN LANGUAGES.[1]

1889.

THREE years ago I was one of those who gathered in the Sanders Theatre to commemorate the two hundred and fiftieth anniversary of a college founded to perpetuate living learning chiefly by the help of three dead languages, the Hebrew, the Greek, and the Latin. I have given them that order of precedence which they had in the minds of those our pious founders. The Hebrew came first because they believed that it had been spoken by God himself, and that it would have been the common speech of mankind but for the judicial invention of the modern languages at Shinar. Greek came next because the New Testament was written in that tongue, and Latin last as the interpreter between scholars. Of the men who stood about that fateful cradle swung from bough of the primeval forest, there were probably few who believed that a book written in any living language could itself live.

For nearly two hundred years no modern language was continuously and systematically taught here. In the latter half of the last century a stray

[1] An address before the Modern Language Association of America.

Frenchman was caught now and then, and kept as long as he could endure the baiting of his pupils. After failing as a teacher of his mother-tongue, he commonly turned dancing-master, a calling which public opinion seems to have put on the same intellectual level with the other. Whatever haphazard teaching of French there may have been was, no doubt, for the benefit of those youth of the better classes who might go abroad after taking their degrees. By hook or by crook some enthusiasts managed to learn German,[1] but there was no official teacher before Dr. Follen about sixty years ago. When at last a chair of French and Spanish was established, it was rather with an eye to commerce than to culture.

It indicates a very remarkable, and, I think, wholesome change in our way of looking at things that I should now be addressing a numerous Society composed wholly of men engaged in teaching thoroughly and scientifically the very languages once deemed unworthy to be taught at all except as a social accomplishment or as a commercial subsidiary. There are now, I believe, as many teachers in that single department of Harvard College as sufficed for the entire undergraduate course when I took my first degree. And this change has taken place within two generations.

---

[1] Mr. George Bancroft told me that he learned German of Professor Sydney Willard, who, himself self-taught, had no notion of its pronunciation. One instructor in French we had, a little more than a century ago, in Albert Gallatin, a Swiss, afterwards eminent as a teacher in statesmanship and diplomacy. There was no regularly appointed tutor in French before 1806.

Τῷ δ' ἤδη δύο μὲν γενεαὶ μερόπων ἀνθρώπων
'Εφθίαθ'.

I make this familiar quotation for two reasons:
because Chapman translates μερόπων "divers-lan-
guaged," which is apt for our occasion, and because it enables me to make an easier transition
to what I am about to say ; namely, that I rise to
address you not without a certain feeling of em-
barrassment. For every man is. more or less consciously, the prisoner of his date, and I must
confess that I was a great while in emancipating
myself from the formula which prescribed the
Greek and Latin Classics as the canonical books
of that infallible Church of Culture outside of
which there could be no salvation, — none, at least,
that was orthodox. Indeed, I am not sure that I
have wholly emancipated myself even yet. The
old phrases (for mere phrases they had mostly
come to be) still sing in my ears with a pleasing if
not a prevailing enchantment.

The traditions which had dictated this formula
were of long standing and of eminent respectability. They dated back to the *exemplaria Græca*
of Horace. For centuries the languages which
served men for all the occasions of private life
were put under a ban, and the revival of learning
extended this outlawry to the literature, such as it
was, that had found vent through them. Even
the authors of that literature tacitly admitted the
justice of such condemnation when they used the
word *Latin* as meaning language *par excellence*,
just as the Newfoundlanders say *fish* when they

mean cod. They could be witty, eloquent, pathetic, poetical, competent, in a word, to every demand of their daily lives, in their mother-tongue, as the Greeks and Romans had been in theirs, but all this would not do; what was so embalmed would not keep. All the prudent and forethoughtful among them accordingly were careful to put their thoughts and fancies, or what with them supplied the place of these commodities, into Latin as the one infallible pickle. They forgot the salt, to be sure, an ingredient which the author alone can furnish. For it is not the language in which a man writes, but what he has been able to make that language say or sing, that resists decay. Yet men were naturally a great while in reaching this conviction. They thought it was not good form, as the phrase is, to be pleased with what, and what alone, really touched them home. The reproach — *at vestri proavi* — rang deterrent in their ears. The author of " Partonopeus de Blois," it is true, plucks up a proper spirit : —

> " Cil clerc dient que n'est pas sens
> Qu'escrive estoire d'antif tens,
> Quant je nes escris en latin,
> Et que je perc mon tans enfin;
> Cil le perdent qui ne font rien
> Moult plus que je ne fac le mien."

And the sarcasm of the last couplet was more biting even than the author thought it. Those moderns who wrote in Latin truly *ne faisoient rien*, for I cannot recollect any work of the kind that has in any sense survived as literature, unless it be the " Epistolæ Obscurorum Virorum " (whose Latin is a part of its humor) and a few short copies of verse, as they used, aptly enough, to be called. Milton's foreign correspondence as Secretary for the Commonwealth was probably the latest instance of the use of Latin in diplomacy.

You all remember Du Bellay's eloquent protest, " I cannot sufficiently blame the foolish arrogance and temerity of some of our nation, who, being least of all Greeks or Latins, depreciate and reject with a more than Stoic brow everything written in French, and I cannot sufficiently wonder at the strange opinion of some learned men, who think our vernacular incapable of all good literature and erudition." When this was said, Montaigne was already sixteen years old, and, not to speak of the great mass of verse and prose then dormant in manuscript, France had produced in Rabelais a great humorist and strangely open-eyed thinker. and in Villon a poet who had written at least one immortal poem, which still touches us with that painless sense of the *lachrymæ rerum* so consoling in poetry and the burthen of which

> " Ou sont les neiges d'antan ? "

falters and fades away in the ear like the last stroke of Beauty's passing-bell. I must not let you forget that Du Bellay had formed himself on the classics, and that he insists on the assiduous study of them. " Devour them," he says, " not in order to imitate, but to turn them into blood and nutriment." And surely this always has been and always will be their true use.

It was not long before the living languages justified their right to exist by producing a living
literature, but as the knowledge of Greek and Latin
was the exclusive privilege of a class, that class
naturally made an obstinate defence of its vested
rights.   Nor was it less natural that men like Bacon, who felt that he was speaking to the civilized
world, and lesser men, who fancied themselves
charged with a pressing message to it, should
choose to utter themselves in the only tongue that
was cosmopolitan.   But already such books as had
more than a provincial meaning, though written in
what the learned still looked on as *patois*, were
beginning to be translated into the other European
languages.   The invention of printing had insensibly but surely enlarged the audience which genius
addresses.   That there were persons in England
who had learned something of French, Italian,
Spanish, and of High and Low Dutch three centuries ago is shown by the dramatists of the day,
but the speech of the foreigner was still generally
regarded as something noxious.   Later generations
shared the prejudice of sturdy Abbot Samson, who
confirmed the manor of Thorpe " cuidam Anglico
natione . . . de cujus fidelitate plenius confidebat
quia bonus agricola erat *et quia nesciebat loqui
Gallice.*"   This was in 1182, but there is a still
more amusing instance of the same prejudice so
lately as 1668.   " Erasmus hath also a notable
story of a man of the same age, an Italian, that
had never been in Germany, and yet he spake
the German tongue most elegantly, being as one

possessed of the Devil ; notwithstanding was cured by a Physician that administered a medicine which expelled an infinite number of *worms*, whereby *he was also freed of his knowledge of the German tongue.*" [1] Dr. Ramesey seems in doubt whether the vermin or the language were the greater deliverance.

Even after it could no longer be maintained that no masterpiece could be written in a modern language, it was affirmed, and on very plausible grounds, that no masterpiece of style could be so written unless after sedulous study of the ancient and especially of the Grecian models. This may have been partially, but was it entirely true ? Were those elements of the human mind which tease it with the longing for perfection in literary workmanship peculiar to the Greeks ? Before the new birth of letters, Dante (though the general scheme of his great poem be rather mechanical than organic) had given proof of a style, which, where it is best, is so parsimonious in the number of its words, so goldenly sufficient in the value of them, that we must go back to Tacitus for a comparison, and perhaps not even to him for a parallel. But Dante was a great genius, and language curtsies to its natural kings. I will take a humbler instance, the *Chant-fable* of " Aucassin and Nicolete," rippling into song, and subsiding from it unconsciously as a brook. Leaving out the episode of the King of

---

[1] From a treatise on worms by William Ramesey, physician in ordinary to Charles II., which contains some very direct hints of the modern germ-theory of disease.

Torclore, evidently thrust in for the groundlings, what is there like it for that unpremeditated charm which is beyond the reach of literary artifice and perhaps does not survive the early maidenhood of language? If this be not style, then there is something better than style. And is there anything so like the best epigrams of Meleager in grace of natural feeling, in the fine tact which says all and leaves it said unblurred by afterthought, as some little snatches of song by nameless French minstrels of five centuries ago ?

It is instructive that, only fifty years after Du Bellay wrote the passage I have quoted, Bishop Hall was indirectly praising Sidney for having learned in France and brought back with him to England that very specialty of culture which we are told can only be got in ancient Greece or, at second hand, in ancient Rome. Speaking of some nameless rhymer, he says of him that

> " He knows the grace of that new elegance
> Which sweet Philisides fetched late from France."

And did not Spenser (whose earliest essay in verse seems to have been translated from Du Bellay) form himself on French and Italian models? Did not Chaucer and Gower, the shapers of our tongue, draw from the same sources? Does not Higgins tell us in the " Mirrour for Magistrates " that Buckhurst, Phaer, Tuberville, Golding, and Gascoygne imitated Marot? Did not Montaigne prompt Bacon to his Essays and Browne (unconsciously and indirectly, it may be) to his " Religio Medici " ? Did not Skelton borrow his so-called

Skeltonian measure from France? Is not the verse
of " Paradise Lost " moulded on that of the " Divina Commedia"? Did not Dryden's prose and
Pope's verse profit by Parisian example? Nay, in
our own time, is it not whispered that more than
one of our masters of style in English, and they,
too, among the chief apostles of classic culture,
owe more of this mastery to Paris than to Athens
or Rome? I am not going to renew the Battle of
the Books, nor would I be understood as question-
ing the rightful place so long held by ancient and
especially by Greek literature as an element of culture and that the most fruitful. But I hold this
evening a brief for the Modern Languages, and am
bound to put their case in as fair a light as I conscientiously can. Your kindness has put me in a
position where I am forced to reconsider my opinions and to discover, if I can, how far prejudice
and tradition have had a hand in forming them.

I will not say with the Emperor Charles V. that
a man is as many men as he knows languages, and
still less with Lord Burleigh that such polyglottism
is but " to have one meat served in divers dishes."
But I think that to know the literature of another
language, whether dead or living matters not, gives
us the prime benefits of foreign travel. It relieves
us from what Richard Lassels aptly calls a " moral
Excommunication : " it greatly widens the mind's
range of view, and therefore of comparison, thus
strengthening the judicial faculty ; and it teaches
us to consider the relations of things to each other
and to some general scheme rather than to our-

selves ; above all, it enlarges æsthetic charity. It
has seemed to me also that a foreign language,
quite as much as a dead one, has the advantage of
putting whatever is written in it at just such a distance as is needed for a proper mental perspective.
No doubt this strangeness, this novelty, adds much
to the pleasure we feel in reading the literature of
other languages than our own. It plays the part
of poet for us by putting familiar things in an un-
accustomed way so deftly that we feel as if we had
gained another sense and had ourselves a share in
the sorcery that is practised on us. The words of
our mother-tongue have been worn smooth by so
often rubbing against our lips or minds, while the
alien word has all the subtle emphasis and beauty
of some new-minted coin of ancient Syracuse. In
our critical estimates we should be on our guard
against this charm.

In reading such books as chiefly deserve to be
read in any foreign language, it is wise to translate
consciously and in words as we read. There is
no such help to a fuller mastery of our vernacular. It compels us to such a choosing and testing,
to so nice a discrimination of sound, propriety, position, and shade of meaning, that we now first
learn the secret of the words we have been using
or misusing all our lives, and are gradually made
aware that to set forth even the plainest matter, as
it should be set forth, is not only a very difficult
thing, calling for thought and practice, but an
affair of conscience as well. Translating teaches
us as nothing else can, not only that there is a best

way, but that it is the only way. Those who have
tried it know too well how easy it is to grasp the
verbal meaning of a sentence or of a verse. That
is the bird in the hand. The real meaning, the
soul of it, that which makes it literature and not
jargon, *that* is the bird in the bush which tanta-
lizes and stimulates with the vanishing glimpses we
catch of it as it flits from one to another lurking-
place, —

> " Et fugit ad salices et se cupit ante videri."

After all, I am driven back to my Virgil again,
you see, for the happiest expression of what I was
trying to say. It was these shy allurements and
provocations of Omar Khayyám's Persian which led
Fitzgerald to many a peerless phrase and made an
original poet of him in the very act of translating.
I cite this instance merely by way of hint that as
a spur to the mind, as an open-sesame to the trea-
sures of our native vocabulary, the study of a living language (for literary, not linguistic, ends)
may serve as well as that of any which we rather
inaptly call dead.

We are told that perfection of form can be
learned only of the Greeks, and it is certainly true
that many among them attained to, or developed
out of some hereditary germ of aptitude, a sense
of proportion and of the helpful relation of parts
to the whole organism which other races mostly
grope after in vain. Spenser, in the enthusiasm
of his new Platonism, tells us that " *Soul* is form,
and doth the body make," and no doubt this is
true of the highest artistic genius. Form without

soul, the most obsequious observance of the unities, the most perfect *à priori* adjustment of parts, is a lifeless thing, like those machines of perpetual motion admirable in every way but one — that they will not go. I believe that I understand and value form as much as I should, but I also believe that some of those who have insisted most strongly on its supreme worth as the shaping soul of a work of art have imprisoned the word " soul " in a single one of its many meanings and the soul itself in a single one of its many functions. For the soul is not only that which gives form, but that which gives life, the mysterious and pervasive essence always in itself beautiful, not always so in the shapes which it informs, but even then full of infinite suggestion. In literature it is what we call genius, an insoluble ingredient which kindles, lights, inspires, and transmits impulsion to other minds, wakens energies in them hitherto latent, and makes them startlingly aware that they too may be parts of the controlling purpose of the world. A book may be great in other ways than as a lesson in form, and it may be for other qualities that it is most precious to us. Is it nothing, then, to have conversed with genius ? Goethe's " Iphigenie " is far more perfect in form than his " Faust," which is indeed but a succession of scenes strung together on a thread of moral or dramatic purpose, yet it is " Faust " that we read and hold dear alike for its meaning and for the delight it gives us. And if we talk of classics ; what, then, is a classic, if it be not a book that forever delights, inspires, and surprises, — in which, and in ourselves, by its help, we make new discoveries every day? What book has so warmly embosomed itself in the mind and memory of men as the Iliad? And yet surely not by its perfection in form so much as by the stately simplicity of its style, by its pathetic truth to nature, for so loose and discursive is its plan as to have supplied plausible argument for a diversity of authorship. What work of classic antiquity has given the *bransle*, as he would have called it, to more fruitful thinking than the Essays of Montaigne, the most planless of men who ever looked before and after, a chaos indeed, but a chaos swarming with germs of evolution? There have been men of genius, like Emerson, richly seminative for other minds ; like Browning, full of wholesome ferment for other minds, though wholly destitute of any proper sense of form. Yet perhaps those portions of their writings where their genius has precipitated itself in perfect, if detached and unrelated crystals, flashing back the light of our common day tinged with the diviner hue of their own nature, are and will continue to be a more precious and fecund possession of mankind than many works more praiseworthy as wholes, but in which the vitality is less abounding, or seems so because more evenly distributed and therefore less capable of giving that electric shock which thrills through every fibre of the soul.

But Samuel Daniel, an Elizabethan poet less valued now than many an inferior man, has said something to my purpose far better than I could

have said it. Nor is he a suspicious witness, for
he is himself a master of style. He had studied
the art of writing, and his diction has accordingly
been less obscured by time than that of most of his
contemporaries. He knew his classics, too, and his
dullest work is the tragedy of "Cleopatra" shaped
on a classic model, presumably Seneca, certainly
not the best. But he had modern instincts and a
conviction that the later generations of men had
also their rights, among others that of speaking
their minds in such forms as were most congenial
to them. In answer to some one who had de-
nounced the use of rhyme as barbarous, he wrote
his "Defence of Rhyme," a monument of noble
and yet impassioned prose. In this he says, "Suffer the world to enjoy that which it knows and
what it likes, seeing whatsoever form of words doth
move delight, and sway the affections of men, in
what Scythian sort soever it be disposed and uttered, that is true number, measure, eloquence, and
the perfection of speech." I think that Daniel's instinct guided him to a half-truth, which he as usual
believed to include the other half also. For I have
observed that truth is the only object of man's
ardent pursuit of which every one is convinced
that he, and he alone, has got the whole.

I am not sure that Form, which is the artistic
sense of decorum controlling the coördination of
parts and ensuring their harmonious subservience
to a common end, can be learned at all, whether of
the Greeks or elsewhere. I am not sure that even
Style (a lower form of the same faculty or quality,

whichever it be), which has to do with the perfection of the parts themselves, and whose triumph it is to produce the greatest effect with the least possible expenditure of material, — I am not sure that even this can be taught in any school. If Sterne had been asked where he got that style which, when he lets it alone, is as perfect as any that I know, if Goldsmith had been asked where he got his, so equable, so easy without being unduly familiar, might they not have answered with the maiden in the ballad, —

> "I gat it in my mither's wame,
> Where ye 'll get never the like " ?

But even though the susceptibility of art must be inborn, yet skill in the practical application of it to use may be increased, — best by practice, and very far next best by example. Assuming, however, that either Form or Style is to be had without the intervention of our good fairy, we can get them, or at least a wholesome misgiving that they exist and are of serious import, from the French, as Sir Philip Sidney and so many others have done, as not a few are doing now. It is for other and greater virtues that I would frequent the Greeks.

Browning, in the preface to his translation of the "Agamemnon," says bluntly, as is his wont, " learning Greek teaches Greek and nothing else." One is sometimes tempted to think that it teaches some other language far harder than Greek when one tries to read his translation. Matthew Arnold, on the other hand, was never weary of insisting that the *grand style* could be best learned of the Greeks, if not of them only. I think it may be taught, or, at least, fruitfully suggested, in other ways. Thirty odd years ago I brought home with me from Nuremberg photographs of Peter Fischer's statuettes of the twelve apostles. These I used to show to my pupils and ask for a guess at their size. The invariable answer was "larger than life." They were really about eighteen inches high, and this grandiose effect was wrought by simplicity of treatment, dignity of pose, a large unfretted sweep of drapery. This object-lesson I found more telling than much argument and exhortation. I am glad that Arnold should have been so insistent, he said so many admirable things in maintaining his thesis. But I question the validity of single verses, or even of three or four, as examples of style, whether grand or other, and I think he would have made an opponent very uncomfortable who should have ventured to discuss Homer with as little knowledge of Greek as he himself apparently had of Old French when he commented on the " Chanson de Roland." He cites a passage from the poem and gives in a note an English version of it which is translated, not from the original, but from the French rendering by Génin who was himself on no very intimate terms with the archaisms of his mother-tongue. With what he says of the poem I have little fault to find. It is said with his usual urbane discretion and marked by his usual steadiness of insight. But I must protest when he quotes four lines, apt as they are for his purpose, as an adequate sample, and then compares them with a most musically pathetic passage from Homer. Who is there that could escape undiminished from such a comparison? Nor do I think that he appreciated as he should one quality of the poem which is essentially Homeric : I mean its invigorating energy, the exhilaration of manhood and courage that exhales from it, the same that Sidney felt in ·· Chevy Chase." I believe we should judge a book rather by its total effect than by the adequacy of special parts, and is not this effect moral as well as æsthetic? If we speak of style, surely that is like good breeding, not fortuitous, but characteristic, the key which gives the pitch of the whole tune. If I should set some of the epithets with which Achilles lays Agamemnon about the ears in the first book of the Iliad in contrast with the dispute between Roland and Oliver about blowing the olifaunt, I am not sure that Homer would win the prize of higher breeding. Or shall I cite Hecuba's

$$\tau\text{o}\tilde{\upsilon}\ \dot{\epsilon}\gamma\grave{\omega}\ \mu\acute{\epsilon}\sigma\text{o}\nu\ \tilde{\eta}\pi\alpha\rho\ \check{\epsilon}\chi\text{o}\iota\mu\iota$$
$$\text{'}\text{E}\sigma\theta\acute{\epsilon}\mu\epsilon\nu\alpha\iota\ \pi\rho\text{o}\sigma\phi\tilde{\upsilon}\sigma\alpha\ ?$$

The "Chanson de Roland" is to me a very interesting and inspiring poem, certainly not to be named with the Iliad for purely literary charm, but equipped with the same moral qualities that have made that poem dearer to mankind than any other. When I am ·· moved more than with a trumpet." I care not greatly whether it be blown by Greek or Norman breath.

And this brings me back to the application of what I quoted just now from Daniel. There seems to be a tendency of late to value literature and even poetry for their usefulness as courses of moral philosophy or metaphysics, or as exercises to put and keep the mental muscles in training. Perhaps the highest praise of a book is that it sets us thinking, but surely the next highest praise is that it ransoms us from thought. Milton tells us that he thought Spenser " a better teacher than Scotus or Aquinas," but did he prize him less that he lectured in a garden of Alcina? To give pleasure merely is one, and not the lowest, function of whatever deserves to be called literature. Culture, which means the opening and refining of the faculties, is an excellent thing, perhaps the best, but there are other things to be had of the Muses which are also good in their kind. Refined pleasure is refining pleasure too, and teaches something in her way, though she be no proper schooldame. In my weaker moments I revert with a sigh, half deprecation, half relief, to the old notion of literature as holiday, as

"The world's sweet inn from care and wearisome turmoil."

Shall I make the ignominious confession that I relish Skelton's "Philip Sparowe," pet of Skelton's Maistres Jane, or parts of it, inferior though it be in form, almost as much as that more fortunate pet of Lesbia? There is a wonderful joy in it to chase away ennui, though it may not thrill our intellectual sensibility like its Latin prototype.

And in this mood the Modern Languages add largely to our resources. It may be wrong to be happy unless in the grand style, but it is perilously agreeable. And shall we say that the literature of the last three centuries is incompetent to put a healthy strain upon the more strenuous faculties of the mind? That it does not appeal to and satisfy the mind's loftier desires? That Dante, Machiavelli, Montaigne, Bacon, Shakespeare, Cervantes, Pascal, Calderon, Lessing, and he of Weimar in whom Carlyle and so many others have found their University, — that none of these set our thinking gear in motion to as good purpose as any ancient of them all? Is it less instructive to study the growth of modern ideas than of ancient? Is the awakening of the modern world to consciousness and its first tentative, then fuller, then rapturous expression of it, like

> — " the new-abashed nightingale
> That stinteth first when she beginneth sing,''
>
> " Till the fledged notes at length forsake their nests,
> Fluttering in wanton shoals,''

less interesting or less instructive to us because it finds a readier way to our sympathy through a postern which we cannot help leaving sometimes on the latch, than through the ceremonious portal of classical prescription? Goethe went to the root of the matter when he said, " people are always talking of the study of the ancients; yet what does this mean but apply yourself to the actual world and seek to express it, since this is what the ancients also did when they were alive?" That " when they were *alive*" has an unconscious sarcasm in it. I am not ashamed to confess that the

first stammerings of our English speech have a pathetic charm for me which I miss in the wiser and
ampler utterances of a tongue, not only foreign to
me as modern languages are foreign, but thickened
in its more delicate articulations by the palsying
touch of Time.   And from the native woodnotes
of many modern lands, from what it was once the
fashion to call the rude beginnings of their literature, my fancy carries away, I think, something as
precious as Greek or Latin could have made it.
Where shall I find the piteous and irreparable poverty of the parvenu so poignantly typified as in the
" Lai de l'Oiselet " ?   Where the secret password
of all poetry with so haunting a memory as in
" Count Arnaldos," —

> " Yo no digo esta cancion
> Sino a quien conmigo va " ?

It is always wise to eliminate the personal equation from our judgments of literature as of other
things that nearly concern us.   But what is so
subtle, so elusive, so inapprehensible as this *folle
du logis?*   Are we to be suspicious of a book's
good character in proportion as it appeals more
vividly to our own private consciousness and experience?   How are we to know to how many it
may be making the same appeal?   Is there no
resource, then, but to go back humbly to the old
quod semper, quod ubique, quod ab omnibus, and
to accept nothing as orthodox literature on which
the elder centuries have not laid their consecrating
hands?   The truth is, perhaps, that in reading
ancient literature many elements of false judgment,

partly involved in the personal equation, are inoperative, or seem to be so, which, when we read a more nearly neighboring literature, it is wellnigh impossible to neutralize. Did not a part of Matthew Arnold's preference for the verses of Homer, with the thunder-roll of which he sent poor old Thuroldus about his business, spring from a secret persuasion of their more noble harmony, their more ear-bewitching canorousness? And yet he no doubt recited those verses in a fashion which would have disqualified them as barbarously for the ear of an ancient Greek as if they had been borrowed of Thuroldus himself. Do we not see here the personal fallacy's eartip? I fancy if we could call up the old *jongleur* and bid him sing to us, accompanied by his *vielle*, we should find in his verses a plaintive and not unimpressive melody such as so strangely moves one in the untutored song of the Tuscan peasant heard afar across the sun-steeped fields with its prolonged fondling of the assonants. There is no question about what is supreme in literature. The difference between what is best and what is next best is immense; it is felt instinctively; it is a difference not of degree but of kind. And yet may we not without lese-majesty say of books what Ferdinand says of women, —

> " for several virtues
> Have I liked several women; never any
> With so full soul but some defect in her
> Did quarrel with the noblest grace she owed
> And put it to the foil " ?

In growing old one grows less fanatically punc-

tual in the practice of those austerities of taste
which make too constant demands on our self-denial.   The ages have made up their minds about
the ancients.   While they are doing it about the
moderns (and they are sometimes a little long
about it, having the whole of time before them),
may we not allow ourselves to take an honest
pleasure in literature far from the highest, if you
will, in point of form, not so far in point of substance, if it comply more kindly with our mood or
quicken it with oppugnancy according to our need ?
There are books in all modern languages which
fulfil these conditions as perfectly as any, however
sacred by their antiquity, can do.   Were the men
of the Middle Ages so altogether wrong in prefer-
ring Ovid because his sentiment was more in touch
with their own, so that he seemed more neighborly ?
Or the earlier dramatists in overestimating Seneca
for the same reason ?   Whether it be from natural
predisposition or from some occult influence of the
time, there are men who find in the literature of
modern Europe a stimulus and a satisfaction which
Athens and Rome deny them.   If these books do
not give so keen an intellectual delight as the
more consummate art and more musical voice of
Athens enabled her to give, yet they establish and
maintain, I am more than half willing to believe,
more intimate and confiding relations with us.
They open new views, they liberalize us as only an
acquaintance with the infinite diversity of men's
minds and judgments can do, they stimulate to
thought or tease the fancy with suggestion, and in

short do fairly well whatever a good book is expected to do, what ancient literature did at the
Revival of Learning, with an effect like that which
the reading of Chapman's Homer had upon Keats.
And we must not forget that the best result of
this study of the ancients was the begetting of the
moderns, though Dante somehow contrived to get
born with no help from the Greek Hera and little
more from the Roman Lucina. " 'T is an unjust
way of compute," says Sir Thomas Browne, " to
magnify a weak head for some Latin abilities, and
to undervalue a solid judgment because he knows
not the geneaology of Hector."

As implements of education, the modern books
have some advantages of their own. I am told,
and I believe, that there is a considerable number
of not uningenuous youths, who, whether from
natural inaptitude or want of hereditary predisposition, are honestly bored by Greek and Latin, and
who yet would take a wholesome and vivifying interest in what was nearer to their habitual modes
of thought and association. I would not take this
for granted, I would give the horse a chance at
the ancient springs before I came to the conclusion
that he would not drink. No doubt, the greater
difficulty of the ancient languages is believed by
many to be a prime recommendation of them as
challenging the more strenuous qualities of the
mind. I think there are grounds for this belief,
and was accordingly pleased to learn the other day
that my eldest grandson was taking kindly to his
Homer. I had rather he should choose Greek

than any modern tongue, and I say this as a hint that I am making allowance for the personal equation. The wise gods have put difficulty between man and everything that is worth having. But where the mind is of softer fibre, and less eager of emprise, may it not be prudent to open and make easy every avenue that leads to literature, even though it may not directly lead to those summits that tax the mind and muscle only to reward the climber at last with the repose of a more ethereal air?

May we not conclude that modern literature, and the modern languages as the way to it, should have a more important place assigned to them in our courses of instruction, assigned to them moreover as equals in dignity, except so far as age may justly add to it, and no longer to be made to feel themselves inferior by being put below the salt? That must depend on the way they are taught, and this on the competence and conscience of those who teach them. Already a very great advance has been made. The modern languages have nothing more of which to complain. There are nearly as many professors and assistants employed in teaching them at Harvard now as there were students of them when I was in college. Students did I say? I meant boys who consented to spend an hour with the professor three times a week for the express purpose of evading study. Some of us learned so much that we could say " How do you do?" in several languages, and we learned little more. The real impediment was that we were kept forever in the elementary stage, that we could look forward to no literature that would have given significance to the languages and made them beneficent. It is very different now, and with the number of teachers the number of students has more than proportionally increased. And the reason is not far to seek. The study has been made more serious, more thorough, and therefore more inspiring. And it is getting to be understood that as a training of the faculties, the comparative philology, at least, of the modern languages may be made as serviceable as that of the ancient. The classical superstitions of the English race made them especially behindhand in this direction, and it was long our shame that we must go to the Germans to be taught the rudiments of our mother tongue. This is no longer true. Anglo-Saxon, Gothic, Old High and Middle High German and Icelandic are all taught, not only here, but in all our chief centres of learning. When I first became interested in Old French I made a surprising discovery. If the books which I took from the College Library had been bound with gilt or yellow edges, those edges stuck together as, when so ornamented, they are wont to do till the leaves have been turned. No one had ever opened those books before.

> " I was the first that ever burst
> Into that silent sea."

Old French is now one of the regular courses of instruction, and not only is the language taught, but its literature as well. Remembering what I remember, it seems to me a wonderful thing that I should have lived to see a poem in Old French edited by a young American scholar (present here this evening) and printed in the journal of this Society, a journal in every way creditable to the scholarship of the country. Nor, as an illustration of the same advance in another language, should we forget Dr. Fay's admirable Concordance of the " Divina Commedia." But a more gratifying illustration than any is the existence and fruitful activity of this Association itself, and this select concourse before me which brings scholars together from all parts of the land, to stimulate them by personal commerce with men of kindred pursuits, and to unite so many scattered energies in a single force controlled by a common and invigorated purpose.

We have every reason to congratulate ourselves on the progress the modern languages have made as well in academic as in popular consideration. They are now taught (as they could not formerly be taught) in a way that demands toil and thought of the student, as Greek and Latin, and they only, used to be taught, and they also open the way to higher intellectual joys, to pastures new and not the worse for being so, as Greek and Latin, and they only, used to do. Surely many-sidedness is the very essence of culture, and it matters less what a man learns than how he learns it. The day will come, nay, it is dawning already, when it will be understood that the masterpieces of whatever language are not to be classed by an arbitrary standard, but stand on the same level in virtue of being

masterpieces; that thought, imagination, and fancy
may make even a *patois* acceptable to scholars;
that the poets of all climes and of all ages " sing
to one clear harp in divers tones; " and that the
masters of prose and the masters of verse in all
tongues teach the same lesson and exact the same
fee.

I began by saying that I had no wish to renew
the Battle of the Books. I cannot bring myself to
look upon the literatures of the ancient and modern worlds as antagonists, but rather as friendly
rivals in the effort to tear as many as may be
from the barbarizing plutolatry which seems to
be so rapidly supplanting the worship of what
alone is lovely and enduring. No, they are not
antagonists, but by their points of disparity, of
likeness, or contrast, they can be best understood,
perhaps understood only through each other. The
scholar must have them both, but may not he who
has not leisure to be a scholar find profit even in
the lesser of the two, if that only be attainable?
Have I admitted that one is the lesser? *O matre
pulchra filia pulchrior* is perhaps what I should
say here.

If I did not rejoice in the wonderful advance
made in the comparative philology of the modern
languages, I should not have the face to be standing here. But neither should I if I shrank from
saying what I believed to be the truth, whether here
or elsewhere. I think that the purely linguistic
side in the teaching of them seems in the way to
get more than its fitting share. I insist only that

in our college courses this should be a separate
study, and that, good as it is in itself, it should, in
the scheme of general instruction, be restrained to
its own function as the guide to something better.
And that something better is Literature.   Let us
rescue ourselves from what Milton calls " these
grammatic flats and shallows."   The blossoms of
language have certainly as much value as its roots;
for if the roots secrete food and thereby transmit
life to the plant, yet the joyous consummation of
that life is in the blossoms, which alone bear the
seeds that distribute and renew it in other growths.
Exercise is good for the muscles of mind and to
keep it well in hand for work, but the true end of
Culture is to give it play, a thing quite as needful.

What I would urge, therefore, is that no invidi-
ous distinction should be made between the Old
Learning and the New, but that students, due
regard being had to their temperaments and faculties, should be encouraged to take the course in
modern languages as being quite as good in point
of mental discipline as any other, if pursued with
the same thoroughness and to the same end.   And
that end is Literature, for there language first
attains to a full consciousness of its powers and
to the delighted exercise of them.   Literature has
escaped that doom of Shinar which made our
Association possible, and still everywhere speaks in
the universal tongue of civilized man.   And it is
only through this record of Man's joys and sorrows, of his aspirations and failures, of his thought,
his speculation, and his dreams, that we can become

complete men, and learn both what he is and what
he may be, for it is the unconscious autobiography
of mankind. And has no page been added to it
since the last ancient classic author laid down his
pen?

THE PROGRESS OF THE WORLD.[1]

1886.

As at noon every day the captain of a ship tries to learn his whereabouts of the sun, that he may know how much nearer he is to his destined port, and how far he may have been pushed away from his course by the last gale or drifted from it by unsuspected currents, so on board this ship of ours, The Earth, in which that abstract entity we call The World is a passenger, we strive to ascertain, from time to time, with such rude instruments as we possess, what progress we have made and in what direction. It is rather by a kind of dead-reckoning than by taking the height of the Sun of Righteousness, which should be our seamark, that we accomplish this, for such celestial computations are gone somewhat out of fashion. It is only a few scholars and moralists in their silent and solitary observatories that any longer make account of them. We mostly put faith in our statisticians, and the longer they make their columns of figures, the bigger their sums of population, of exports and imports, and of the general output of fairy-gold,

---

[1] This paper was written for an introduction to a work entitled *The World's Progress* (published by Messrs. Gately & O'Gorman, Boston), in which the advance in various departments of intellectual and material activity was described and illustrated.

the more stupidly are we content. Nor are we over-nice in considering the direction of our progress, if only we be satisfied that to-day we are no longer where we were yesterday. Yet the course of this moral thing we call the World is controlled by laws as certain and immutable and by influences as subtle as those which govern with such exquisite precision that of the physical thing we call The Earth, could we only find them out. It has ever been the business of wise men to trace and to illustrate them, of prudent men to allow for and to seek an alliance with them, of good men to conform their lives with them.

Between those observations taken on shipboard and ours there is also this other difference, that those refer always to a fixed, external standard, while for these the standard is internal and fluctuating, so that the point toward which The World is making progress shall seem very different according to the temperament, the fortunes, nay, even the very mood or age of the observer. It may be remarked that Mr. Gladstone and Lord Tennyson are very far from being at one in their judgment of it. Old men in general love not change, and are suspicious of it; while young men are impatient of present conditions and of the slowness of movement to escape from them. Yet change is the very condition of our being and thriving, deliberation and choice that of all secure foothold on the shaky stepping-stones by which we cross the torrent of Circumstances. Is it in the power of any man, whatever his age, to arrive at that equilibrium of temper and judgment without which no even probable estimate of where we are and whither we are tending is possible? Certainly no such trustworthy estimate can be deduced from our inward consciousness or from our outward environments; nor can we, with all our statistics, make ourselves independent of the inextinguishable lamps of heaven. We pile our figures one upon another, even as the builders of Babel their bricks, and the heaven we hope to attain is as far away as ever. It is moral forces that, more than all others, govern the direction and regulate the advance of our affairs, and these forces are as calculable as the Trade Winds or the Gulf Stream.

And yet, though this be so, one of the greatest lessons taught by History is the close relation between the moral and the physical well-being of man. The case of the Ascetics makes but a seeming exception to this law, for they voluntarily denied themselves that bodily comfort which is the chief object of human endeavor, and renunciation is the wholesomest regimen of the soul. If we cannot strike a precise balance and say that the World is better because it is richer now than it was three centuries, or even half a century, ago, we may at least comfort ourselves with the belief that this, if not demonstrably true, is more than probable, and that there is less curable unhappiness, less physical suffering, and therefore less crime, than heretofore. Yet there is no gain without corresponding loss. If the sum of happiness be greater, yet the amount falling to each of us in

the division of it seems to be less. It is noteworthy
that literature, as it becomes more modern, becomes
also more melancholy, and that he who keeps most
constantly to the minor key of hopelessness, or
strikes the deepest note of despair, is surest of at
least momentary acclaim. Nay, do not some
sources of happiness flow less full or cease to flow
as settlement and sanitation advance, even as the
feeders of our streams are dried by the massacre
of our forests? We cannot have a new boulevard
in Florence unless at sacrifice of those ancient city-
walls in which inspiring memories had for so many
ages built their nests and reared their broods of
song. Did not the plague, brooded and hatched
in those smotherers of fresh air, the slits that thor-
oughfared the older town, give us the Decameron?
And was the price too high? We cannot widen
and ventilate the streets of Rome without grievous
wrong to the city that we loved, and yet it is well
to remember that this city too had built itself out
of and upon the ruins of that nobler Rome which
gave it all the wizard hold it had on our imagination. The Social Science Congress rejoices in
changes that bring tears to the eyes of the painter
and the poet. Alas! we cannot have a world made
expressly for Mr. Ruskin, nor keep it if we could,
more 's the pity! Are we to confess, then, that the
World grows less lovable as it grows more convenient and comfortable? that beauty flees before the
step of the Social Reformer as the wild pensioners
of Nature before the pioneers? that the lion will lie
down with the lamb sooner than picturesqueness

with health and prosperity? Morally, no doubt, we are bound to consider the Greatest Good of the Greatest Number, but there is something in us, *vagula, blandula*, that refuses, and rightly refuses, to be Benthamized; that asks itself in a timid whisper, "Is it so certain, then, that the Greatest Good is also the Highest? and has it been to the Greatest or to the Smallest Number that man has been most indebted?" For myself, while I admit, because I cannot help it, certain great and manifest improvements in the general well-being, I cannot stifle a suspicion that the Modern Spirit, to whose tune we are marching so cheerily, may have borrowed of the Pied Piper of Hamelin the instrument whence he draws such bewitching music. Having made this confession, I shall do my best to write in a becoming spirit the Introduction that is asked of me, and to make my antiquated portico as little unharmonious as I can with the modern building to which it leads.

But, before we enter upon a consideration of the Progress of the World, we must take a glance at that of the Globe on whose surface what we call the World came into being, rests, and has grown to what we see. This Globe is not, as we are informed, a perfect sphere, but slightly flattened at the poles; and in like manner this World is by no means a perfect world, though it be not quite so easy, as in the other case, to say where or why it is not. For it there is no moon-mirror in which to study its own profile. Perhaps it would be wise to ask ourselves now and then whether the fault may not be in the nature of man, after all, rather than anywhere else. So far as he is a social animal, that is, an animal liable in various ways to make his neighbor uncomfortable, it is certainly prudent to remember always that, though his natural impulses may be restrained, or guided, or even improved, yet that they are always there and ready to take the bit in their teeth at the first chance which offers. This might save us a pretty long bill for quack nostrums, since, though no astronomer has ever volunteered to rectify the Earth's outline, there is hardly a man who does not fancy that the World would become and continue just what it should be, if only his patent specific could once be fairly tried. Quacks of genius like Rousseau have sometimes persuaded to the experiment of their panaceas, but always with detriment to the patient's constitution. We are long in learning the lesson of Medea's cauldron.

The Earth, fortunately, is beyond the reach of our wisdom, and, like the other shining creatures of God, whirls her sphere and brings about her appointed seasons in happy obedience to laws for which she is not responsible and which she cannot tinker. Beginning as a nebulous nucleus of fiery gases, a luminous thistle-down blown about the barren wastes of space, then slowly shrinking, compacting, growing solid, and cooling at the rind, our planet was forced into a system with others like it, some smaller, some vastly greater than itself, and, in its struggle with overmastering forces, having the Moon wrenched from it to be its night-lamp and the timer of its tides.   Then slowly, slowly, it became capable of sustaining living organisms, rising by long and infinitesimal gradations, symbolically rehearsed again, it is said, by the child in embryo, from the simplest to the more complex, from merely animated matter to matter informed with Soul, and, in Man, sometimes controlled by reason.   The imagination grows giddy as it looks downwards along the rounds of the ladder lost, save a short stretch of it, in distance below, by which life has climbed from the zoöphyte to Plato, to Newton, to Michael Angelo, to Shakespeare. During the inconceivable æons implied in these processes, the Earth has gone through many vicissitudes, unrecorded save in the gigantic runes of Geology, the *graffiti* of Pluto and Neptune, which man, having painfully fashioned a key to them, is spelling out letter by letter, arranging as syllables, as words, as sentences, and at last reading as coherent narrative.   Every one of these records is the mortuary inscription of an Epoch or a Cycle, but the last word of every one is *Resurgam*.   They point backwards to such endless files of centuries that the poor six thousand years of our hieratic reckoning are dwindled to a hair-breadth, and our students of the rocks and stars, like the drunken man of Esdras, disdain the smaller change of temporal computation, and rattle off their millions as carelessly as Congress in dealing with our National strongbox.   Nor has this sudden accession of secular wealth made them any more careful of the humbler interests of their neighbors than it is

wont to make other *nouveaux riches*. A malig-
nant astronomer has lately done his best to prove
that the sun's stock of fuel cannot hold out more
than seventeen millions of years. Is, then, that
assurance of an earthly immortality which has hitherto sustained poets through cold and hunger and
Philistine indifference, to be fobbed off at last with
so beggarly a pittance as this? Let us hope for
better things.

Though these memories of the rocks and mountains and ocean-beds seem to belittle and abbreviate
man, yet it is nothing so; for, till he came, the
universe, so far as we can explore and know it, had
neither eyes, nor ears, nor tongue, nor any dimmest
consciousness of its own being. This antiquity
has been the gift of modern science; and the brain
of man has been the hour-glass that gave to these
regardless sands of Time, running to waste through
the dreaming fingers of idle Oblivion, the measure
and standard of their own duration. It is the cun-
ning of man that has delineated the great dial-plate
of the heavens; his mind that looks before and
after, and can tell the unwitting stars where they
were at any moment of the unmeasured past, where
they will be at any moment of the unmeasurable future. Though he cannot loose the bands of Orion,
he can weigh them to the uttermost scruple; though
he cannot bind the sweet influences of the Pleiades,
he knows upon what eyes of mortal men they are
shed, and at what moment, though by himself un-
seen. Shut in his study, he can look at the New
Moon with lovers at the Antipodes. If Science have

made men seem ephemeral as midges, she has conferred a great benefit on humanity by endowing collective Man with something of that longæval dignity which she has compelled the individual to renounce.   He is no longer the creature of yesterday, but the crowning product and heir of ages so countless as to make Time a sharer in the grandeur of that immensity to which Astronomy has dilated the bounds of Space.   And who shall reproach her with having put far away from us the homely and neighborly heaven of unlettered faith, when she has opened such a playground for the outings of speculation, and noted in her guide-book so many spacious inns for the refreshment of the disembodied spirit on its travels, so many and so wondrous *magnalia* for its curiosity and instruction?   To me it seems not unreasonable to find a reinforcement of optimism, a renewal of courage and hope, in the modern theory that man has mounted to what he is from the lowest step of potentiality, through toilsome grades of ever-expanding existence, even though it have been by a spiral stairway, mainly dark or dusty, with loopholes at long intervals only, and these granting but a narrow and one-sided view.   The protoplasmic germ to which it was incalculable promotion to become a stomach, has it not, out of the resources with which God had endowed it, been able to develop the brain of Darwin, who should write its biography?   Even Theology is showing signs that she is getting ready to exchange a man who fell in Adam for a man risen out of nonentity and still rising through that aspir-

ing virtue in his veins which is spurred onwards
and upwards by the very inaccessibility of what he
sees above him.

But I have kept Man cooling his heels too long
in these antechambers of his larger life. He becomes more interesting to us, and we are more willing to admit his claim of kinship with us, in proportion as he has entered upon a larger share of
his inheritance. His condition of nonage and apprenticeship was unconscionably long; but there
was no escape, since it was Nature that had drawn
his indentures. Till he had learned to write, what
we seem to know of him is hypothetical merely,
and he was dull at his pothooks and trammels.
The book which you have before you enables you
to see, in brief but sufficient compendium, the advances made by mankind in the various lines of
human enterprise and development, which, leading
away from a single centre, gradually enlarge the
circumference of his activity and the horizon of
his intelligent desires and hopes. We begin with
Man where our records of him begin, in the rude
memorials of himself he has unwittingly left us.
Fancy and conjecture may find ample and instructive entertainment if they try to conceive him as he
was at first, — a dweller in the natural shelter of
caverns, fashioning, on rainy days, spear-heads and
arrow-tips of flint, or fishing-hooks of the bones of
the very prey that was to be their victim. Perhaps
the need of even a natural roof implies that he had
already learned, as no other animal has ever learned,
to cover nature's waterproof suit with some kind

of clothing. Next, we follow him as he emerges from the isolation of Family to the wider relations of Tribe, Nation, Community, State. Before even the simplest of these latter organizations could be possible, he must have invented language; and this could have been no improvisation. Indeed, would we conceive how slow his progress must have been, we have only to consider the multitude of inventions, like the wheel, the lever, the bow, the sling, every one of which a child now uses — perhaps by hereditary instinct — with as little forethought as if they were natural limbs. Yet all these and countless others waited till a genius came along to make them servants of man; and surely Nature is sparing of genius. He was a Kepler who first counted the fingers of one hand; he a Galileo who added those of the other, and gave us the decimal system; he a Newton who divined the possibility of numbering his toes also and arriving at the score. By and by another great inventor devised the tally, and property in flocks and herds, the first riches, became secure because numerable and matter of record. Nay, if we consider that every man we meet walking is a miracle (for it is nothing less than this so to evade the law of gravitation as to balance himself on one foot at every step), and that every infant must give two or three years to the acquiring of this art, we shall the more easily reconcile ourselves with the prolonged periods of preparation and training which our present civilization presupposes.

Pope has fancied man a pupil of the lower ani-

mals, learning of the little nautilus to sail; and no
doubt it is a fruitful characteristic of man that he
is clever enough to take and to profit by those nods
and winks that are thrown away upon the blind
horses of creation. These, too, — if we are to
suppose him to stand in need of them, — he is capable of expanding and perfecting till the original
germ be lost in the medley of variation and accre-
tion. This skill in emendation, this faculty of im-
proving on his models and achievements, is what
happily distinguishes him. The bee builds as he
began in Eden, — a perfect architect from the first,
— only accommodating the structure of his cells to
circumstances when he cannot help it. The nautilus spreads his cobweb sail as the first navigator
of his race spread his. The tradition of the natural
caverns in which his ancestor found shelter and
warmth may have taught the troglodyte to burrow
in cliffs of softer stone; but the first tree under
which man sought refuge from a shower must have
read him a more convincing lecture on the advantages of a permanent roof than any that Vitruvius
or Palladio could have furnished him. The first
tree-trunk he saw floating downstream might well
be his earliest lesson in shipbuilding; the first
wooden bowl dropped into the brook by a careless
girl might suggest to some master mind the advantage of hollowing the log, to give it buoyancy, balance, and capacity. But, from the mere conception of shelter, man was beckoned onwards by the
longing to complete and crown use with beauty,
till, from the seed of the wattled hovel, sprang at

last, in supreme loveliness, the Parthenon and the Cathedral, in architrave or arch, still filially renewing the idealized features of the primitive ancestor. The rude dugout or coracle of the primæval mariner has grown into a palace on the sea, a city on the inconstant billows dancing, that carries its sails and fair winds in its own entrails, and pushes prevailingly against the very breast of the storm.

Man is the only animal that has given proof of invention in the highest sense, that is, not as a mere fence against the blasts of discomfort, or as a lightener of his drudgery, but as a minister of beauty; the only one who of Nature's chains has made his ornaments, and of her obstacles the stepping-stones of his advance. Other creatures show, or seem to show, pleasure in bright colors, or sensibility to modulated sounds; but only Man has combined and harmonized those into picture and these into music. The eye of the ox is a placid mirror of the meadow into which he gazes, unconscious as the dull pool that images the magnificence of sky and mountain or the various grace of growth upon its borders. The eye of man is a window, not to the sense only, but to the soul behind the sense; it has memory and desire, nor will let him rest till he have reproduced and made permanent some semblance of what engaged his fancy or wakened his imagination. Even among cave-dwellers, we find, scratched on the bones from which they had gnawed the flesh, outlines of the mastodon and of a combat of stags, — crude endeavors after art, deeply suggestive, in their intention, of some im-

possible Snyders or Landseer beguiling the impulse he could neither stifle nor satisfy.

Though he cannot create, man reflects the Creative Power through his sense of Form, Order, and
Proportion, — the abstractions by which that Power
is most vividly manifested.   He has the supreme
faculty of organization.   Multiply the bison in-
definitely, and the result is still a herd: multiply
man, and he organizes himself, arranging himself,
more or less rudely, by some process of moral
gravitation, in a form of polity, or groping clumsily in search thereof; he cannot long remain mob,
even if he would.   Other creatures are endowed
with that kind of crystallized reason which we call
instinct.   In the highest types of man alone does
reason continue ductile and versatile, enabling him
to supplement or multiply his natural organs and
powers by artificial contrivances, and thus to realize the dreams and fables of his remote progeni-
tors.   We write no more fairy tales, because the
facts of our every-day lives are more full of mar-
vel than they.   Other creatures have curiosity;
but it stops short in the vagueness of wonder, nor
pushes on, like that of man, to discovery.   Other
animals stare; man looks.   Many are gregarious,
some social, and some — as ants, bees, and beavers
— dwell in communities and socialize their labor;
man only has devised a society which, imperfect in
many ways and wasteful as it is, contains within
itself the elements of growth and amelioration.   It
is a suggestive fact that, within the historic period,
no new animal has been tamed to the service or

companionship of man. Only he can record his memory, and so fund his experience for the benefit of his posterity; only he is capable of being bored, — the sharpest spur to enterprise, to action, to the contempt of life. Captaincy among the lower animals means superior strength and the cheap courage that comes of it: among men it means brains, it means, above all, character; and they have contrived, by making Law supreme, to make all men alike strong. Dogs know when they have done wrong, but their moral standard is the displeasure of their master; man has invented, or, at any rate, developed, conscience, — the only infallible detective, the only impeccable judge, the only executioner with whom no reprieve avails. The endeavor has been made to distinguish man from the brutes by defining him as the only animal that laughs, that has learned the uses of fire, and what not. We might be tempted to call him the only animal who thinks he is thinking when he is merely ruminating. But I conceive his truer and higher distinction to be that he alone has the gift, or, rather, is laid under the ennobling necessity, of conceiving and formulating an ideal; which means that he alone may be the servant and steward of the Divine Beauty.

In these volumes the reader will find all that he can reasonably wish to know about prehistoric or historic man, and about the floating globe on which he dwells, treated at sufficient length by competent persons, each dealing with that part of the subject to which his special studies had been devoted.

He will learn how far and in what directions man
has advanced, how much of his inheritance he has
subdued and occupied, and with what results. He
will learn what is meant by the familiar phrase
that man is "the heir of all the ages," and how
nobly exacting are the duties and privileges implied
in it. He will observe how certain races have
been endowed with special qualities and aptitudes;
as, the Greeks for art, in its most widely inclusive
sense; the Jews, for commerce and (strange para-
dox) for the higher divinations of the soul; the
Romans, for civil and military administration;
our own, for polity and the planting of colonies.
He will trace back astronomy to Chaldæa, theog-
ony to Babylonia, and metaphysical speculation to
India. In certain directions he will find no advance, as in literature and sculpture, since the
Greeks; in ethics, since the Sermon on the Mount.
He will see some races that have been seemingly
able to spin a civilization, as the spider his web,
out of their own entrails, and yet none that has
not borrowed, few which have not a tradition that
the seeds of culture were brought to them from
abroad. This will lead him to think how large a
part commerce must have had in the civilizing
process, and that, before commerce was possible,
communities must have existed of sufficient duration and stability to produce more than they could
consume, and therefore to desire profitable ex-
changes. It should be encouraging, then, to see,
as we now see, the carrier-doves of commerce
spreading their white wings over every ocean and

every land-locked sea. For, if they sometimes bear with them the germs of contagious social evils, they bear also those of good; and we should despair of humanity did we not believe that these strike a deeper and more enduring root, till they crowd out their noxious rivals and occupy all the soil. But if the adventurer into strange lands too often carry darkness with him, he seldom fails to bring back light; for nothing is more certain than that the mind widens with its wider circuit, and is liberalized by contact with various races, religions, and forms of civilization. It was said of old, "Men shall run to and fro, and knowledge shall be increased." We have a striking instance of this in the Crusaders, who, though they did not realize their dream of permanent conquest, came home, if not more human, at least more cosmopolitan, which is a long stride towards becoming so, and unwittingly brought with them the seeds of that freer thinking which slowly conquered for Man that freedom to think which was to emancipate Europe and make America possible. But we should always bear in mind the wise saying of Goethe, that "whatever emancipates our minds without giving us the mastery of ourselves is destructive." And, if Commerce have enriched us in many ways, both spiritually and materially, I cannot let it go without a sigh for the sentimental wrong it has unconsciously done us in bringing about that prosaic uniformity in the costume, both of mind and body, which unhappily distinguishes the modern from that ancient world, to print whose obituary, one

might say, was the first employment of Guten-
berg's types.

If the history of the world show us Man slowly
rising to a higher conception and more adequate
fulfilment of his destiny, it also shows us the sadder
spectacle of empires that have perished and now
lie buried under the decay of their own monuments.
Worse than this, it shows us that higher forms of
civilization may be overwhelmed and supplanted by
lower forms; that some families of men, like the
pure negro, are incapable of civilization from their
own resources, and relapse into savagery when left
to themselves, as in Hayti. Nay, members even
of the higher and more self-sufficing races are
never beyond danger of this relapse when the
wholesome influences and restraints of organized
society are withdrawn. Examples of this are only
too common; as, in armies after a rout, in great
cities under the paralysis of pestilence, and in the
mutineers of the Bounty. The last instance sup-
plies us also with a consoling illustration of the
force of hereditary impulse and the value of character; since the sole survivor, John Adams, was
able, with the Bible behind him, to piece together
again the fragments of society into a patriarchal
community that revived the legend of Arcadia.
The fact that civilization is, after all, built on so
sandy a foundation as the nature of man, that it
is exposed to all the storms that lie in wait for the
fortunes of man, should make us more sensible of
that duty of unremitting vigilance which is needful
for its safeguard.

In casting the figure of the World's future, many new elements, many disturbing forces, must be taken into account. First of all is Democracy, which, within the memory of men yet living, has assumed almost the privilege of a Law of Nature, and seems to be making constant advances towards universal dominion. Its ideal is to substitute the interest of the many for that of the few as the test of what is wise in polity and administration, and the opinion of the many for that of the few as the rule of conduct in public affairs. That the interest of the many is the object of whatever social organization man has hitherto been able to effect seems unquestionable; whether their opinions are so safe a guide as the opinions of the few, and whether it will ever be possible, or wise if possible, to substitute the one for the other in the hegemony of the World, is a question still open for debate. Whether there was ever such a thing as a Social Contract or not, as has been somewhat otiosely discussed, this, at least, is certain, — that the basis of all Society is the putting of the force of all at the disposal of all, by means of some arrangement assented to by all, for the protection of all, and this under certain prescribed forms. This has always been, consciously or unconsciously, the object for which men have striven, and which they have more or less clumsily accomplished. The State — some established Order of Things, under whatever name — has always been, and must always be, the supremely important thing; because in it the interests of all are invested, by it the duties of all imposed and exacted. In point of fact, though it be often strangely overlooked, the claim to any selfish hereditary privilege because you are born a man is as absurd as the same claim because you are born a noble. In a last analysis, there is but one natural right; and that is the right of superior force. This primary right, having been found unworkable in practice, has been deposited, for the convenience of all, with the State, from which, as the maker, guardian, and executor of Law, and as a common fund for the use of all, the rights of each are derived, and man thus made as free as he can be without harm to his neighbor. It was this surrender of private jurisdiction which made civilization possible, and keeps it so. The abrogation of the right of private war has done more to secure the rights of man, properly understood, — and, consequently, for his well-being. — than all the theories spun from the brain of the most subtle speculator, who, finding himself cramped by the actual conditions of life, fancies it as easy to make a better world than God intended, as it has been proved difficult to keep in running order the world that man has made out of his fragmentary conception of the divine thought. The great peril of democracy is, that the assertion of private right should be pushed to the obscuring of the superior obligation of public duty.

The pluralizing in his single person, by the Editor of the Newspaper, of the offices once divided among the Church. the University, and the Courts of Law, is one of the most striking phenomena of

modern times in democratized countries, and is
calculated to inspire thoughtful men with some
distrust. Such pretension to omniscience and to
the functions it involves has not been seen since
the days of Voltaire, and even he never aspired to
anything beyond the privilege of issuing his own
private notes and not the bonds on which the credit
of the Universe depends. The Church, the University, and the Courts taught at least under the
guidance of some extrinsic standard of Authority,
or of Experience, or of Tradition, but what may
be the outcome of a world edited subjectively every
morning is matter of alarming conjecture. Anon-
ymousness also evades responsibility. But it is
encouraging to note that the higher type of editor
is coming every day to a fuller sense of the meaning of his many-sided calling, and that the newspaper itself is really beginning to furnish an instructive epitome of contemporary culture in all its
branches, which, if it cannot supply the place of
more thorough and special training, may inspire in
some an appetite for it, and prevent others from
suffering, so much as they otherwise might, by the
want of it. Moreover, the power to influence public opinion is cumulative, gathering slowly but
surely to the abler and more scrupulous conductors
of the press, and it is observable that Wisdom
generally comes to stay, while Error is apt to be
but a transitory lodger.

Another very serious factor in the problem of
the future is Socialism. This, it is true, is no
novel phenomenon. Its theory, at least, must have

been dimly conceived by the first man who had little and wanted more, and who found Society guilty of the shortcomings whose cause may have been mainly in himself. Nay, there is dynamite enough in the New Testament, if illegitimately applied, to blow all our existing institutions to atoms. All well-meaning and humane men sympathize with the aims of Lasalle and Karl Marx. All thoughtful men see well-founded and insuperable difficulties in the way of their accomplishment. But the socialism of the closet is a very different thing from that of hordes of unthinking men to whom universal suffrage may give the power of unmaking Order by making Laws. Our federal system gives us a safeguard, however, that is wanting in more centralized governments. Should one State choose to make the experiment of mending its watch by taking out the mainspring, the others can meanwhile look on and take warning by the result. We have already observed a movement towards the introduction of socialistic theories into both State and National legislation, though, if History teach anything, it teaches that the true function of Government is the prevention and remedy of evils so far only as these depend on causes within the reach of law, and that it has lost any proper conception of its duty when it becomes a distributor of alms. Timid people dread the insurrection of Bone and Sinew without seeing that unwise concessions to their unreasoned demands, which include the right to revive private war, will lead inevitably to the revolt of Brain, with consequences far more disastrous to the liberties so painfully won in all the ages during which man has been visible to us. When men formed their first Society, they instinctively recognized, in the Priest, the Lawgiver, or the Great Captain, the supreme fact that Intellect is the divinely appointed lieutenant of God in the government of this World, and in the ordering of man's place in it and of his relations towards it. This viceroy may be deposed, as during the drunkenness of the French Revolution, but out of the very crime will arise the Avenger.

It has seemed to some, and those not the least wise of their generation, that the advance of Science on which we so much plume ourselves was no unmixed good, and that this seemingly gracious benefactress perhaps took away with one hand as much as she gave with the other. We are not yet in a position to compute the results of its influence in modifying human thought and action. That it may be great none doubt who are capable of forming a judgment; and, if long life were for any reason a desirable thing, I can conceive of none more valid than that it might be prolonged till some of these results could be classed and tabulated. I cannot share their fears who are made unhappy by the foreboding that Science is in some unexplained way to take from us our sense of spiritual things. What she may do is to forbid our vulgarizing them by materialistic conceptions of their nature; and in this she will be serving the best interests of Truth and of mankind also. For it is Man's highest distinction and safeguard that he cannot if he would rest satisfied till he have pushed to its full circumference whatever fragmentary arc of truth he has been able to trace with the compasses of his mind. Give to Science her undisputed prerogative in the realm of matter, and she must become, whether she will or no, the tributary of Faith. *Invisibilia enim ipsius [Dei] a creatura mundi per ea quæ facta sunt intellecta.* Whatever else Science may accomplish, she will never contrive to make all men equally tall in body or mind. By labor-saving expedients she may multiply every man's hands by fifty, but she can never find a substitute for the planning and directing head; nor, though she abolish space and time, can she endow electricity and vibration with the higher functions of soul. The more she makes one lobe of the brain Aristotelian, so much more will the other intrigue for an invitation to the banquet of Plato. Theology will find out in good time that there is no atheism at once so stupid and so harmful as the fancying God to be afraid of any knowledge with which He has enabled Man to equip himself. Should the doctrines of Natural Selection, Survival of the Fittest, and Heredity be accepted as Laws of Nature, they must profoundly modify the thought of men and, consequently, their action. But we should remember that it is the privilege and distinction of man to mitigate natural laws, and to make them his partners if he cannot make them his servants. Human nature is too expansive a force to be safely bottled up in any scientific formula, however incontrovertible.

I should be glad to speculate also on the effect of the tendency of population towards great cities; no new thing, but intensified as never before by increased and increasing ease of locomutation. The evil is intensified by the fact that this migration is recruited much more largely from the helpless than from the energetic class of the rural population; and it is not only an evil but a danger where, as with us, suffrage has no precautionary limits. If no remedy be possible, a palliative should be sought in whatever will make the country more entertaining; as in village libraries that may turn solitude into society, and in a more thorough and intelligent teaching of natural history in our public schools. The ploughman who is also a naturalist runs his furrow through the most interesting museum in the world. To discuss the cohesive or disruptive forces of Race and of Nationality might tempt me still to linger, but I have kept the reader quite long enough from the book itself. I have barely touched on several points on which it has roused or quickened thought. So far as the material prosperity of mankind is concerned, the review is by no means discomforting, and as I am one of those who believe that only when the bodily appetites of man are satisfied, does he become first conscious of a spiritual hunger and thirst that demand quite other food to appease them, so we may say, with some confidence, *sicut patribus erit Deus nobis.*

www.ingramcontent.com/pod-product-compliance
Lightning Source LLC
Chambersburg PA
CBHW031109020726
47495CB00007B/2120

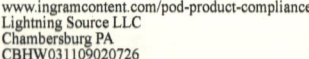